Why Four Gospels?

ARTHUR W. PINK

WIPF & STOCK · Eugene, Oregon

Wipf and Stock Publishers
199 W 8th Ave, Suite 3
Eugene, OR 97401

Why Four Gospels?
By Pink, Arthur W.
ISBN 13: 978-1-60899-786-2
Publication date 7/16/2010
Previously published by Bible Truth Depot, 1921

TABLE OF CONTENTS

Foreword	5
Introduction	7
Matthew's Gospel	25
The Gospel of Mark	59
The Gospel of Luke	87
The Gospel of John	131
Conclusion	171
Appendix	185

FOREWORD.

It is now upwards of twelve years since the writer first read Mr. Andrew Jukes' book on the Gospels, wherein he so ably outlined the various characters, in which the four Evangelists, severally, present the Lord Jesus Christ. Since then we have continued, with ever increasing delight, to trace out for ourself, the various features which are peculiar to each Gospel.

It has been our privilege to give a series of Bible readings on the design and scope of the Gospels, to various companies, both in England and in this country; and many have been the requests for us to publish them in book form. We have hesitated to do this, because Mr. Jukes, fifty years ago, had already dealt with this subject with better success than we could hope to achieve. Since his day, a number of others have written upon the same theme, though not with the same perspecuity and helpfulness. Really, Mr. Jukes covered the ground so thoroughly (at least in its broad outlines) that for any later writer who would present anything approaching a bird's-eye view of the four Gospels, it was well-nigh impossible to avoid going over much of the ground covered by the original pioneer, and repeating much of what he first, under God, set forth to such good effect. It is only because Mr. Jukes' work is unknown to many whom we hope to reach, that we now present these studies to the Christian public. We have worked diligently on the subject for ourself, and have sought to thoroughly assimilate that which we received first from the writing of the above mentioned, while adding, also, our own findings.

In sending forth this little book, much of which has been gathered up from the labors of another, we are reminded of the words of the Apostle Paul to Timothy, his son in the faith: "And the things that thou hast *heard of me* among many witnesses, the same *commit thou* to faithful men" (2 Tim. 2:2). And again: "But continue thou in the things which thou hast learned and hast been assured of, knowing *of whom thou hast learned them*" (2 Tim. 3:14).

We are fully assured that there is very much in the four Gospels which manifest the Divine perfections and distinctive beauties of each one, which has not yet been brought forth by those who have sought to explore their inexhaustible depths; that there is here a wide field for diligent research, and that those who will pursue this study, prayerfully, for themselves, will be richly rewarded for their pains. May it please God to stir up an increasing number of His people to *"search"* this portion of His holy Word which reveal, as nowhere else, the excellencies of His blessed Son, which were so signally displayed by Him during the years that He tabernacled among men.

Arthur W. Pink,
1921.   Swengel, Pa.

INTRODUCTION
WHY FOUR GOSPELS?

WHY FOUR GOSPELS?

WHY four Gospels? It seems strange that such a question needs to be asked at this late date. The New Testament has now been in the hands of the Lord's people for almost two thousand years, and yet, comparatively few seem to grasp the character and scope of its first four books. No part of the Scriptures has been studied more widely than have the four Gospels: innumerable sermons have been preached from them, scores of commentaries have been written upon them, and every two or three years sections from one of the Gospels is assigned as the course for study in our Sunday Schools. Yet, the fact remains, that the peculiar design and character of Matthew, Mark, Luke, and John, is rarely perceived even by those most familiar with their contents.

Why four Gospels? It does not seem to have occurred to the minds of many to ask such a question. That we have four Gospels which treat of the earthly ministry of Christ is universally accepted, but as to *why* we have them, as to *what* they are severally designed to teach, as to their peculiar characteristics, as to their distinctive beauties—these are little discerned and even less appreciated. It is true that each of the four Gospels has much in common to all: each of them deals with the same period of history, each sets forth the teaching and miracles of the Saviour, each describes His death and resurrection. But while the four Evangelists have much in common, each has much that is peculiar to himself, and it is in noting *their variations* that we are brought to see their true meaning and scope and to appreciate their perfections. Just as a course in architecture enables the student to discern the subtle distinctions between the Ionic, the Gothic, and the Corinthian styles—distinctions which are *lost* upon the uninstructed; or, just as a musical training fits one to appreciate the grandeur of a master-production, the loftiness of its theme, the beauty of its chords, the variety of its parts, or its rendition—all lost upon the un-initiated; so the exquisite perfections of the four Gospels are unnoticed, and unknown by those who see in them nothing more than four biographies of Christ.

In carefully reading through the four Gospels it soon becomes apparent to any reflecting mind that in none of them, nor in the four together, do we have anything approaching a *complete biography* of our Saviour's earthly ministry. There are great gaps in His life which none of the Evangelists profess to fill in. After the record of His infancy, nothing whatever is told us about Him till He had reached the age of twelve, and after the brief record which Luke gives of Christ as a boy in the Temple at Jerusalem, followed by the statement that His parents went to Nazareth and that there He was "subject unto them" (Luke 2), nothing further is told us about Him until He had reached the age of thirty. Even when we come to the accounts of His public ministry it is clear that the records are but fragmentary; the Evangelists select only portions of His teachings and describe in detail but a few of His miracles. Concerning the full scope of all that was crowded into His wonderful life, John gives us some idea when he says, "And there are *also* many other things which Jesus did, the which, if they should be written every one, I suppose that even the world itself could not contain the books that should be written" (John 21:25).

If then the Gospels are not complete biographies of Christ, what are they? The first answer must be, Four books inspired, fully inspired, of God; four books written by men moved by the Holy Spirit; books that are true, flawless, perfect. The second answer is that, the four Gospels are so many books, each complete in itself, each of which is written with a *distinctive design,* and that which is included in its pages, and all that is left out, is strictly *subordinated* to that design, according to a principle of selection. In other words, nothing whatever is brought into any one of the Gospels save that which was strictly relevent and pertinent to its peculiar theme and subject, and all that was irrelevent and failed to illustrate and exemplify its theme was excluded. The same plan of *selection* is noticeable in every section of the Holy Scriptures.

Take Genesis as an example. Why is it that the first two thousand years of history are briefly outlined in its first eleven chapters, and that the next three hundred years is spread out over thirty-nine chapters? Why is it that so very little is said about the men who lived *before* the Flood, whereas the lives of Abraham and Isaac, Jacob and Joseph are described in such fulness of detail? Why is it that the Holy Spirit has seen well to depict at greater length the experiences of Joseph in Egypt than He devoted to the Account of Creation? Take, again, the later historical books. A great deal is given us concerning the varied experiences of Abraham's descendants, but little notice is taken of the mighty Nations which were contemporaneous with them. Why is it that *Israel's history* is described at such length, and that of the Egyptians, the Hittites, the Babylonians, the Persians, and the Greeks, is almost entirely ignored? The answer to all of these questions is that, the Holy Spirit *selected* only that which served the purpose before Him. The *purpose* of Genesis is to explain to us the *origin* of that Nation which occupies so prominent a place in the Old Testament Scriptures, hence, the Holy Spirit hurries over, as it were, the centuries before *Abraham* was born, and then proceeds to describe in detail the lives of the fathers from which the Chosen Nation sprang. The same principle obtains in the other books of the Old Testament. Because the Holy Spirit is there setting forth the dealings of God *with Israel*, the other great nations of antiquity are largely ignored, and only come into view at all *as they directly concerned* the Twelve-Tribed people. So it is in the four Gospels: each of the Evangelists was guided by the Spirit to record only that which served to set forth Christ in the particular character in which He was there to be viewed, and that which was *not* in keeping with that particular character was left out. Our meaning will become clearer as the reader proceeds.

Why four Gospels? Because one or two was not sufficient to give a *perfect* presentation of the varied glories of our blessed Lord. Just as no one of the Old Testament typical personages (such as Isaac or Joseph, Moses or David) give an *exhaustive* foreshadowment of our Lord, so, no one of the four Gospels presents a *complete* portrayal of Christ's manifold excellencies. Just as no one or two of the five great offerings appointed by God for Israel (see Lev. 1—6) could, by itself, represent the many-sided sacrifice of Christ, so no one, or two, of the Gospels could, by itself, display fully the varied relationships which the Lord Jesus sustained when He was here upon earth. In a word, *the four Gospels set Christ before us as filling four distinct offices.* We might illustrate it thus. Suppose I was to visit a strange town in which there was an imposing city-hall, and that I was anxious to convey to my friends at home the best possible idea of it. What would I do? I would use my camera to take four different pictures of it, one from each side, and thus my friends would be able to obtain a complete conception of its structure and beauty. Now that is exactly what we have in the four Gospels. Speaking reverently, we may say that the Holy Spirit has photographed the Lord Jesus from four different angles, viewing Him in four different relationships, displaying Him as perfectly discharging the responsibilities of four different offices. And it is impossible to read the Gospels intelligently, to understand their variations, to appreciate their details, to get out of them what we ought, until the reader learns exactly from *which* angle each separate Gospel is viewing Christ, which particular relationship Matthew or Mark shows Him to be discharging, which office Luke or John shows Him to be filling.

The four Gospels alike present to us the person and work of our blessed Saviour, but each one views Him in a distinct relationship, and only that which served to illustrate the separate design which each Evangelist had before him found a place in his Gospel; everything else which was not strictly germane to his immediate purpose was omitted. To make this still more simple we will use another illustration. Suppose that today four men should undertake to write a "life" of ex-president Roosevelt, and that each one designed to present him in a *different* character. Suppose that the first should treat of his *private and domestic* life, the second deal with him as a *sportsman and hunter* of big game, the third depict his *military prowess* and the experiences he had while in the army, while the fourth traced his *political and presidential career*. Now it will be seen at once that these four biographers while writing of the life of the *same* man would, nevertheless, view him in four entirely *different* relationships. Moreover, it will be evident that these biographers would be governed in the *selection* of their material by the *particular purpose* each one had before him: each would include only that which was germane to his own specific viewpoint, and for the same reason each would omit that which was irrelevent. For instance: suppose it was known that Mr. Roosevelt, as a boy, had excelled in gymnastics and athletics *which* of his biographers would mention this fact? Clearly, the second one, who was depicting him as a *sportsman*. Suppose that as a boy Mr. Roosevelt had frequently engaged in fistic encounters, which one would make mention of it? Evidently, the one who was depicting his *military career,* for it would serve to illustrate his *fighting* qualities. Again, suppose that when a college-student Mr. R. had displayed an aptitude for debating, which biographer would refer to it? The fourth, who was treating of his *political and presidential* life. Finally, suppose that from youth upwards, Mr. R. had manifested a marked fondness for children, which of his biographers would refer to it? The first, for he is treating of the ex-president's *private and domestic life*.

The above example may serve to illustrate what we have in the four Gospels. In Matthew, Christ is presented as the Son of David, the King of the Jews, and everything in his narrative centers around this truth. This explains *why* the first Gospel opens with a setting forth of Christ's *royal* genealogy, and *why* in the second chapter mention is made of the journey of the wise men from the East, who came to Jerusalem inquiring "Where is He that is born *King* of the Jews?", and why in chapters five to seven we have what is known as "The Sermon on the Mount" but which, in reality, is the Manifesto of the King, containing an enunciation of the Laws of His Kingdom.

In Mark, Christ is depicted as the Servant of Jehovah, as the One who though equal with God made Himself of no reputation and "took upon Him the form of a servant." Everything in this second Gospel contributes to this central theme, and everything foreign to it is rigidly excluded. This explains *why* there is *no genealogy* recorded in Mark, why Christ is introduced at the beginning of His public ministry (nothing whatever being told us here of His earlier life), and why there are more miracles (deeds of service) detailed here than in any of the other Gospels.

In Luke, Christ is set forth as the Son of Man, as connected with but contrasted from the sons of men, and everything in the narrative serves to bring this out. This explains *why* the third Gospel traces His genealogy back to Adam, the first man, (instead of to Abraham only, as in Matthew), why as the perfect Man He is seen here so frequently in prayer, and why the angels are seen ministering *to* Him, instead of commanded *by* Him as they are in Matthew.

In John, Christ is revealed as the Son of God, and everything in this fourth Gospel is made to illustrate and demonstrate this Divine relationship. This explains *why* in the opening verse we are carried back to a point before time began, and are shown Christ as the Word "in the beginning," with God, and Himself expressly declared to be God; why we get here so many of His Divine titles, as "The only begotten of the Father," the "Lamb of God," the "Light of the world" etc.; why we are told here that prayer should be made in His Name, and why the Holy Spirit is here said to be sent from the Son as well as from the Father.

It is a remarkable fact that this fourfold presentation of Christ in the Gospels was specifically indicated through the Old Testament seers. Conspicuous among the many prophecies of the Old Testament are those which spoke of the coming Messiah under the title of "the Branch." From these we may select four which correspond exactly with the manner in which the Lord Jesus is looked at, respectively, in each of the four Gospels:—

In Jer. 23:5 we read, "Behold, the days come, saith the Lord, that I will raise unto DAVID *a righteous Branch, and a King shall reign* and prosper, and shall execute judgment and justice in the earth." These words fit the first Gospel as glove fits hand.

In Zech. 3:8 we read, "Behold, I will bring forth *My Servant the Branch.*" These words might well be taken as a title for the second Gospel.

In Zech. 6:12 we read, "Behold *the Man* whose

name is *the Branch.*" How accurately this corresponds with Luke's delineation of Christ needs not to be pointed out.

In Isaiah 4:2 we read, "In that day shall *the Branch of the Lord* be beautiful and glorious." Thus, this last quoted of these Messianic predictions, which spoke of the Coming One under the figure of "the Branch," tallies exactly with the fourth Gospel, which portrays our Saviour as the Son of God.

But, not only did Old Testament prophecy anticipate the four chief relationships which Christ sustained on earth, the Old Testament *types* also foreshadowed this fourfold division. In Gen. 2:10 we read "And a river went out of Eden to water the garden; and from thence it was parted, and became into *four heads.*" Note carefully the words "from thence." In Eden itself "the river" was one, but "from thence" it "was *parted*" and became into four heads. There must be some deeply hidden meaning to this, for *why* tell us how many "heads" this river had? The mere historical fact is without interest or value for us, and that the Holy Spirit has condescended to record this detail prepares us to look beneath the surface and seek for some mystical meaning. And surely that is not far to seek. "Eden" suggests to us the Paradise above: the "river" which "watered" it, tells of *Christ* who is the Light and Joy of Heaven. Interpreting this mystic figure, then, we learn that in Heaven Christ was seen in one character only—"The Lord of Glory"—but just as when the "river" left Eden it was parted and became "four heads" and as such thus watered the earth, so, too, the earthly ministry of the Lord Jesus has been, by the Holy Spirit, *"parted into four heads"* in the Four Gospels.

Another Old Testament type which anticipated the fourfold division of Christ's ministry as recorded in the four Gospels may be seen in Ex. 26:31, 32, "And thou shalt make a vail of blue, and purple, and scarlet, and fine twined linen of cunning work: with cherubim shall it be made. And thou shalt hang it upon *four pillars* of shittim wood overlaid with gold: their hooks shall be of gold, upon the four sockets of silver." From Heb. 10:19, 20 we learn that the "veil" foreshadowed the Incarnation, God manifest in flesh—"through the veil, that is to say, *His flesh."* It is surely significant that this "veil" was hung upon *"four* pillars of shittim wood overlaid with gold:" the wood, again, speaking of His humanity, and the gold of His Deity. Just as these "four pillars" served to *display* the beautiful veil, so in the four Gospels we have made manifest the perfections of the only-begotten of the Father tabernacling among men.

In connection with the Scripture last quoted, we may observe one other feature—"with cherubim shall it be made." The veil was ornamented, apparently, with the "cherubim" embroidered upon it in colors of blue, purple, and scarlet. In Ezek. 10: 15, 17 etc. the cherubim are termed "the living creature:" this enables us to identify the "four beasts" of Rev. 4:6, for rendered literally the Greek reads "four living creatures." These "living creatures" or "cherubim" are also *four* in number, and from the description which is furnished of them in Rev. 4:7 it will be found that they correspond, most remarkably with the various characters in which the

WHY FOUR GOSPELS? 19

Lord Jesus Christ is set forth in Matthew, Mark, Luke and John.

"And the first living creature was like a lion, and the second living creature like a calf, and the third living creature had a face as a man, and the fourth living creature was like a flying eagle" (Rev. 4:7). The first cherubim, then, was like "a lion" which reminds us at once of the titles which are used of Christ in Rev. 5:5—*"The Lion* of the Tribe of Judah, the Root of *David."* The lion, which is the king among the beasts is an apt symbol for portraying Christ as He is presented in Matthew's Gospel. Note also that the Lion of the Tribe of Judah is here termed "the Root of *David."* Thus the description given in Rev. 4:7 of the first "cherubim" corresponds exactly with the character in which Christ is set forth in the first Gospel, viz., as "the Son of David," the "King of the Jews." The second cherubim was "like a calf" or "young ox." The young ox aptly symbolizes Christ as He is presented in Mark's Gospel, for just as the ox was the chief animal of *service* in Israel, so in the second Gospel we have Christ presented in lowliness as the perfect "Servant of Jehovah." The third cherubim "had a face *as a man,"* which corresponds with the third Gospel where our Lord's Humanity is in view. The fourth cherubim was "like a flying eagle:" how significant! The first three—the lion, young ox, and man,—all belong to *the earth,* just as each of the first three Gospels each set forth Christ in an earthly relationship; but this fourth cherubim lifts us up *above* the earth, and brings *the heavens* into view! The eagle is the bird that soars the highest and symbolizes the character in which Christ is seen in John's Gospel, viz., as the Son of God. Incidentally we may observe how this description of the four cherubim in Rev. 4:7 *authenticates the arrangement* of the four Gospels as we have them in our Bibles, evidencing the fact that their present *order* is of Divine arrangement as Rev. 4:7 *confirms!*

We would call attention to one other feature ere closing this Introduction and turning to the Gospels themselves. Behold the *wisdom* of God displayed in the selection of the four men whom He employed to write the Gospels. In each one we may discern a peculiar suitability and fitness for his task.

The *instrument* selected by God to write this first Gospel was singularly fitted for the task before him. Matthew is the only one of the four Evangelists who presents Christ in an *official* relationship, namely, as the Messiah and King of Israel, and Matthew himself was the only one of the four who filled an official position; for, unlike Luke, who was by profession a physician, or John who was a fisherman, Matthew was a tax-gatherer in the employ of the Romans. Again; Matthew presents Christ in *Kingdom* connections, as the One who possessed the title to reign over Israel; how fitting, then, that Matthew, who was an officer of and accustomed to look out over a vast empire, should be the one selected for this task. Again; Matthew was a publican. The Romans appointed officials whose duty it was to collect the Jewish taxes. The tax-gatherers were hated by the Jews more bitterly than the Romans themselves. Such a man was Matthew. How feelingly, then, could *he* write of the One who was "hated *without a cause*"! and set forth the Messiah–Saviour as "despised and rejected" by His own nation. Finally, in God appointing this man, who by calling was connected with the Romans, we have a striking anticipation of the grace of God reaching out to the despised Gentiles.

Mark's Gospel sets before us the Servant of Jehovah, God's perfect Workman. And the instrument chosen to write this second Gospel seems to have held an unique position which well fitted him for his task. He was not himself one of the apostles, but was rather *a servant* of an apostle. In 2 Tim. 4:11 we have a scripture which brings this out in a striking manner—"Take Mark, and bring him with thee: for he is profitable to me for the ministry." Thus the one who wrote of our Lord as the Servant of God, was himself one who "ministered" to others!

Luke's Gospel deals with our Lord's Humanity, and presents Him as the Son of Man related to but contrasted from the sons of men. Luke's Gospel is the one which gives us the fullest account of the virgin-birth. Luke's Gospel also reveals more fully than any of the others the fallen and depraved state of human nature. Again; Luke's Gospel is far more *international* in its scope than the other three, and is more Gentilish than Jewish—evidences of this will be presented when we come to examine his Gospel in detail. Now observe the appropriateness of the selection of *Luke* to write *this* Gospel. Who was he? He was neither a fisherman nor a tax-gatherer, but a "physician" (see Col. 4:14), and as such, a student of human nature and a diognostician of the human frame. Moreover, there is good reason to believe that Luke himself was not a Jew but a Gentile, and hence it was peculiarly fitting that *he* should present Christ not as "the Son of David" but as "The Son of *Man*."

John's Gospel presents Christ in the loftiest character of all, setting Him forth in *Divine* relationship, showing that He was the Son of God. This was a task that called for a man of high spirituality, one who was intimate with our Lord in a special manner, one who was gifted with unusual spiritual discernment. And surely John, who was *nearer* to the Saviour than any of the twelve, surely John "the disciple whom Jesus loved," was well chosen. How fitting that the one who leaned on the Master's *bosom* should be the instrument to portray Christ as "The only-begotten Son, which is in the *bosom* of the Father"! Thus may we discern and admire the manifold wisdom of God in equipping the four "Evangelists" for their honorous work.

Ere closing this Introduction we would return once more to our opening query—Why four Gospels? This time we shall give the question a different emphasis. Thus far, we have considered, *Why* four Gospels? And we have seen that the answer is, In order to present the person of Christ in four different characters. But we would now ask, Why *four* Gospels? Why not have reduced them to two or three? Or, why not have added a fifth? Why *four?* God has a wise reason for everything, and we may be assured there is a Divine fitness in the number of the Gospels.

In seeking to answer the question, Why *four* Gospels, we are not left to the uncertainties of speculation or imagination. Scripture is its own interpreter. A study of God's Word reveals the fact (as pointed out by others before us), that in it the *numerals* are used with definite precision and meaning. "Four" is the number of *the earth*. It is, therefore, also, the *world* number. We subjoin a few illustrations of this. There are *four* points to earth's compass—north, east, south, and west. There are *four* seasons to earth's year—spring, summer, autumn, and winter. There are *four* elements connected with our world—earth, air, fire, and water. There have been *four,* and only four, great world-empires—the Babylonian, the Medo–Persian, the Grecian, and the Roman. Scripture divides earth's inhabitants into *four* classes—"kindred, and tongue, and people, and nation" (Rev. 5:9 etc.). In the Parable of the Sower, our Lord divided the field into *four* kinds of soil, and later He said, "the field is *the world.*" The *fourth* commandment has to do with rest from all earth's labors. The *fourth* clause in what is known as the Lord's prayer is, "Thy will be done *on earth.*" And so we might go on. Four is thus the earth number. How fitting, then, that the Holy Spirit should have given us *four* Gospels in which to set forth the *earthly* ministry of the Heavenly One.

MATTHEW'S GOSPEL.

MATTHEW'S GOSPEL.

MATTHEW'S Gospel breaks the long silence that followed the ministry of Malachi the last of the Old Testament prophets. This silence extended for four hundred years, and during that time God was hid from Israel's view. Throughout this period there were no angelic manifestations, no prophet spake for Jehovah, and, though the Chosen People were sorely pressed, yet were there no Divine interpositions on their behalf. For four centuries God shut His people up to His written Word. Again and again had God promised to send the Messiah, and from Malachi's time and onwards the saints of the Lord anxiously awaited the appearing of the predicted One. It is at this point Matthew picks up the thread dropped by the last of the Old Testament prophets. The first purpose of Matthew's Gospel is to present Christ as *the Fulfiller* of the promises made to Israel and the prophecies which related to their Messiah. This is why the word "fulfilled" occurs in Matthew fifteen times, and why there are more quotations from the Old Testament in this first Gospel than in the remaining three put together.

The *position* which Matthew's Gospel occupies in the Sacred Canon indicates its *scope:* it follows immediately after the Old Testament, and stands at the beginning of the New. It is therefore a connecting link between them. Hence it is *transitionary* in its character, and more Jewish than any other book in the New Testament. Matthew reveals God appealing to and dealing with His Old Testament people; presents the Lord Jesus as occupying a distinctively Jewish relationship; and, is the only one of the four Evangelists that records Messiah's express declaration, "I am not sent but unto the lost sheep of the House of Israel" (15:24). The numerical position given to Matthew's Gospel in the Divine library confirms what has just been said, for, being the *fortieth* book it shows us Israel in the place of *probation*, tested by the presence of Messiah in their midst.

Matthew presents the Lord Jesus as Israel's Messiah and King, as well as the One who shall save His people from their sins. The opening sentence gives the key to the book—"The book of the generation of Jesus Christ, the Son of David, the Son of Abraham." Seven times the Lord Jesus is addressed as "Son of David" in this Gospel, and ten times, altogether, is this title found there. "Son of David" connects the Saviour with Israel's *throne*, "Son of Abraham" linking Him with Israel's *land*—Abraham being the one to whom Jehovah first gave the land. But nowhere after the opening verse is this title "Son of Abraham" applied to Christ, for the restoration of the land to Israel is consequent upon their acceptance of Him as their Saviour–King, and that which is made prominent in this first Gospel is the presentation of Christ as *King*—twelve times over is this title here applied to Christ.

Matthew is essentially the *dispensational* Gospel and it is impossible to over-estimate its importance and value. Matthew shows us Christ offered to the Jews, and the *consequences* of their *rejection* of Him, namely, the setting aside of Israel, and God turning in grace to the Gentiles. Rom. 15:8, 9 summarizes

WHY FOUR GOSPELS? 29

the scope of Matthew's Gospel—"Jesus Christ was a minister of the circumcision for the truth of God, to confirm the promises made unto the fathers; *And that the Gentiles might glorify God for His mercy.*" Christ was not only born *of* the Jews, but He was born, first, *to* the Jews, so that in the language of their prophet they could exclaim, *"Unto us a Child is born, unto us a Son is given"* (Isa. 9:6). Matthew's Gospel explains why Israel, in the later books of the New Testament, is seen temporally cast off by God, and why He is now taking out from the Gentiles a people for His name; in other words, it makes known why, in the present dispensation, the Church has superseded the Jewish theocracy. It supplies the key to God's dealings with the earth in this Age: without a workable knowledge of this first Gospel it is well-nigh impossible to understand the remaining portions of the New Testament. We turn now to consider some of the outstanding features and peculiar characteristics of Matthew's Gospel.

The first thing which arrests our attention is the opening verse. God, in His tender grace, has hung the key right over the entrance. The opening verse is that which unlocks the contents of this Gospel—"The book of the generation of Jesus Christ, the Son of David, the Son of Abraham." The first five English words here are but two in the Greek—"Biblos geneseos." These two words indicate the peculiarly *Jewish* character of the earlier portions of this Gospel, for it is an Old Testament expression. It is noteworthy that this expression which commences the New Testament is found almost at the beginning of the first book in the Old Testament, for in Gen. 5:1 we read, "This is the book of the generations of Adam." We need hardly say that this word "**gen-**

eration" signifies *the history of*. These two "books"
—the book of the generations of Adam, and the book
of the generation of Jesus Christ—might well be
termed the Book of Death and the Book of Life. Not
only does the whole Bible center around these two
books, but the sum of human destiny also. How
strikingly this expression, found at the beginning of
Genesis and the beginning of Matthew, brings out
the *Unity* of the two Testaments!

In the book of Genesis we have eleven different
"generations" or histories enumerated, beginning
with the "generations of the heavens and the earth,"
and closing with the "generations of Jacob"—see
2:4: 5:1: 6:9: 10:1: 11:10: 11:27: 25:12: 25:19:
36:1: 36:9: 37:2—thus dividing the first book of
the Bible into twelve sections, twelve being the number of Divine government, which is what is before
us in Genesis—God in sovereign government. From
Exodus to Daniel we find government entrusted, instrumentally, to Israel, and from Daniel onwards it
is in the hands of the Gentiles: but in Genesis we
antedate the Jewish theocracy, and there government
is found directly in the hands of God, *hence its
twelvefold division*. Twice more, namely, in Num.
3:1 and Ruth 4:18, do we get this expression "the
generation of," making in the Old Testament thirteen in all, which is the number of *apostasy*, for that
is all the Law revealed! But, as we have seen, this
expression occurs once more (and there for the last
time in Holy Writ) in the opening verse of the
New Testament, thus making fourteen in all, and
the fourteenth is "the book of the generation of
Jesus Christ." How profoundly significant and
suggestive this is! Fourteen is 2 x 7, and two signifies (among its other meanings) contrast or dif-

ference, and seven is the number of perfection and completeness—and what a *complete difference* the Coming of Jesus Christ made!

"The book of the generation of Jesus Christ, *the Son of David, the Son of Abraham*" (Matt. 1:1). These titles of our Saviour have, at least, a threefold significance. In the first place, both of them connect Him with *Israel:* "Son of David" linking Him with Israel's *Throne,* and "Son of Abraham" with Israel's *Land.* In the second place, "Son of David" *limits* Him to Israel, whereas "Son of Abraham" is wider in its scope, reaching forth to the *Gentiles,* for God's original promise was that in Abraham "shall all the families of the earth be blessed" (Gen. 12:3). In the third place, as Dr. W. L. Tucker has pointed out, these titles correspond exactly with the twofold (structural) division of Matthew's Gospel.* Up to 4:16 all is Introductory, and 4:17 opens the first division of the book, reading, *"From that time* Jesus began to preach, and to say, Repent: for the Kingdom of heaven is at hand." This section treats of the Official ministry of Christ and presents Him as "the Son of David." The second section commences at 16:21 and reads, *"From that time forth* Jesus began to show unto His disciples, how that He must go unto Jerusalem, and suffer many things of the elders and chief priests and scribes, and be *killed,* and be raised again the third day." This section treats, primarily, of the *Sacrificial* work of Christ, and views Him as "the Son of Abraham," typified, of old, by Isaac—laid on the altar.

Having dwelt at some length on the opening verse

---

*Dr. Tucker calls attention to the literary divisions of Matthew's Gospel: the *dispensational* break occurring at the close of chapter 12.

of our Gospel, we may next notice that the remainder of the chapter down to the end of verse 17 is occupied with the Genealogy of Jesus Christ. The prime significance of this is worthy of our closest attention, for it fixes with certainty the character and dominant theme of this Gospel. The very first book of the New Testament opens with a long list of names! What a proof that no un-inspired man composed it! But God's thoughts and ways are ever different from ours, and ever perfect too. The reason for this Genealogy is not far to seek. As we have seen, the opening sentence of Matthew contains the key to the book, intimating plainly that Christ is here viewed, first, in a Jewish relationship, fully entitled to sit on David's Throne. How then is His *title* established? By showing that, according to the flesh, He belonged to the *royal* tribe: by setting forth His Kingly line of descent. A King's title to occupy the throne depends not on the public ballot, but lies in his blood rights. Therefore, the first thing which the Holy Spirit does in this Gospel is to give us the Royal Genealogy of the Messiah, showing that as a lineal descendant of David He was fully entitled to Israel's Throne.

The Genealogy recorded in Matt. 1 gives us not merely the *human* ancestry of Christ, but, particularly, His *royal* line of descent, this being one of the essential features which differentiates it from the Genealogy recorded in Luke 3. The fundamental design of Matt. 1:1-17 is to prove Christ's right to reign as King of the Jews. This is why the genealogy is traced no further back than Abraham, he being the father of the Hebrew people. This is why, in the opening verse, the order is "Jesus Christ, the Son of David, the Son of Abraham," instead of

WHY FOUR GOSPELS? 33

"the Son of Abraham, the Son of David" as might be expected from the order which immediately follows, for there we start with Abraham and work *up* to David. Why, then, is this order *reversed* in the opening verse? The answer must be that David comes first because it is *the Kingly line* which is here being emphasised! This also explains why, in verse 2 we read "Abraham begat Isaac; and Isaac begat Jacob, and Jacob begat Judah and his brethren." Why should *Judah* alone be here singled out for mention from the twelve sons of Jacob? Why not have said "Jacob begat Reuben and his brethren"? for he was Jacob's "firstborn." If it be objected that the birthright was transferred from Reuben to Joseph, then we ask, why not have said "Jacob begat Joseph"? especially as Joseph was his favorite son. The answer is, Because Judah was *the royal* tribe, and it is the *Kingly* line which is here before us. Again; in verse 6 we read, "And Jesse begat David *the king:* and David *the king* begat Solomon of her that had been the wife of Uriah." Of all those who reigned over Israel whose names are here recorded in Matthew 1, David is the only one that is denominated "King," and he, twice over in the same verse! Why is this, except to bring *David* into special prominence, and thus show us *the significance* of the title given to our Lord in the opening verse—"the Son *of David."*

There are many interesting features of this Genealogy which we must now pass over, but its *numerical arrangement* calls for a few brief comments. The Genealogy is divided into three parts: the first section, running from Abraham to David, may be termed the period of *Preparation;* the second section, running from Solomon to the Babylonian captivity, may be called the period of *Degeneration;* while the third period, running from the Babylonian captivity till the Birth of Christ, may be named the period of *Expectation*. The numeral three signifies, in Scripture, *manifestation,* and how appropriate this arrangement was here, for not until Christ appears is God's purpose concerning Abraham and his seed fully manifested. Each of these three sections in the Royal Genealogy contains fourteen generations, which is 2 x 7, two signifying (among its slightly varied meanings) testimony or competent witness, and seven standing for perfection. Again we may admire the consonancy of these numerals in this genealogy of Christ, for only in Him do we get *perfect testimony*—the "Faithful and True Witness." Finally, be it observed, that 14 x 3 gives us 42 generations in all from Abraham to Christ, or 7 x 6, seven signifying perfection, and six being the number of man, so that Christ—the forty-second from Abraham—brings us to *the Perfect Man!!* How microscopically perfect is the Word of God!

"And Jacob begat Joseph the husband of Mary, of whom was born Jesus, who is called Christ" (Matt. 1:16). Matthew does not connect Joseph and Jesus as father and son, but departs from the usual phraseology of the genealogy so as to indicate the peculiarity, the uniqueness, of the Saviour's birth. Abraham might begat Isaac, and Isaac begat Jacob, but Joseph the husband of Mary did not begat Jesus, instead, we read, "Now the birth of Jesus Christ was on this wise: when as His mother Mary was espoused to Joseph, *before they came together,* she was found with child of the Holy Spirit" (1:18). As Isaiah had foretold (7:14) seven hundred years before, Messiah was to be born of "the virgin." But

WHY FOUR GOSPELS? 35

a virgin had no *right* to Israel's throne, but Joseph *had* this right, being a direct descendant of David, and so through Joseph, His legal father (for be it remembered that betrothal was as binding with the Jews as marriage is with us) the Lord Jesus secured His rights, according to the flesh, to be King of the Jews.

Coming now to Matt. 2 we may observe that we have in this chapter an incident recorded which is entirely passed over by the other Evangelists, but which is peculiarly appropriate in this first Gospel. This incident is the visit of the wise men who came from the East to honor and worship the Christ Child. The details which the Holy Spirit gives us of this visit strikingly illustrate the distinctive character and scope of Matthew's Gospel. This chapter opens as follows, "Now when Jesus was born in Bethlehem of Judea in the days of Herod the King, behold, there came wise men from the east to Jerusalem, Saying, Where is He that is born King of the Jews? for we have seen His star in the east, and are come to worship Him." Notice, these wise men came not inquiring, "Where is He that is born the Saviour of the world?", nor, "Where is the Word now incarnate?", but instead, "Where is He that is born *King of the Jews?*" The fact that Mark, Luke and John are entirely silent about this, and the fact that Matthew's Gospel *does* record it, is surely proof positive that this First Gospel presents Christ in a distinctively *Jewish relationship*. The evidence for this is cumulative: there is first the peculiar expression with which Matthew opens—"the book of the generation of," which is an Old Testament expression, and met with nowhere else in the New Testament; there is the first title which is given to Christ in this Gospel—"Son of David;" there is the Royal Genealogy which immediately follows; and now there is the record of the visit of the wise men, saying, "Where is He that is born King of the Jews?" Thus has the Spirit of God made so plain and prominent the peculiarly Jewish character of the opening chapters of Matthew's Gospel that none save those who are blinded by prejudice can fail to see its true dispensational place. Thus, too, has He rendered excuseless the foolish agitation which is now, in certain quarters, being raised, and which tends only to confuse and confound.

But there is far more in Matt. 2 than the recognition of Christ as the rightful King of the Jews. The incident therein narrated contains a foreshadowment of the reception which Christ was to meet with here in the world, anticipating the end from the beginning. What we find here in Matt. 2 is really a prophetic outline of the whole course of Matthew's Gospel. First, we have the affirmation that the Lord Jesus was born "King of the Jews;" then we have the fact that Christ is found not in Jerusalem, the royal city, but outside of it; then we have the blindness and indifference of the Jews to the presence of David's Son in their midst—seen in the fact that, first, His own people were *unaware* that the Messiah was now there among them, and second, in *their failure* to accompany the wise men as they left Jerusalem seeking the young Child; then we are shown strangers from a far-distant land with a heart for the Saviour, seeking Him out and worshipping Him; finally, we learn of the civil ruler filled with hatred and seeking His life. Thus, the incident as a whole marvellously foreshadowed Christ's rejection by the Jews and His acceptance by the Gentiles. Thus do we find epitomized here the whole burden of Matthew's Gospel, the special purpose of which is to show Christ presenting Himself to Israel, Israel's rejection of Him, with the consequent result of God setting Israel aside for a season, and reaching out in grace to the despised Gentiles.

Next we read, "And when they were departed, behold the angel of the Lord appeareth to Joseph in a dream, saying, Arise, and take the young Child and His mother, and flee into Egypt, and be thou there until I bring thee word: for Herod will seek the young Child to destroy Him" (2:13). Observe that it is *Joseph* and not Mary that figures so prominently in the first two chapters of Matthew, for it was not through His mother, but through His legal father that the Lord Jesus acquired His title to David's throne—compare Matt. 1:20, where Joseph is termed "son of David"! It should also be pointed out that Matthew is, again, the only one of the four Evangelists to record this journey into Egypt, and the subsequent return to Palestine. This is profoundly suggestive, and strikingly in accord with the special design of this First Gospel, for it shows how Israel's Messiah took the very same place as where Israel's history as a Nation began!

"But when Herod was dead, behold, an angel of the Lord appeareth in a dream to Joseph in Egypt, Saying, Arise, and take the young Child and His mother, and go into the land of Israel: for they are dead which sought the young Child's life. And he arose, and took the young Child and His mother, and came into the land of Israel" (2:19-21). Once more we discover another line which brings out the peculiarly Jewish character of Matthew's delineation of Christ. This is the only place in the New Testament where Palestine is termed "the land of Israel," and it is significantly proclaimed as such here in connection with Israel's King, for it is not until He shall set up His Throne in Jerusalem that Palestine shall become in fact, as it has so long been in promise, "the Land of Israel." Yet how tragically suggestive is the statement that immediately follows here, and which closes Matt. 2. No sooner do we read of "the land of Israel" than we find "But" as the very next word, and in Scripture, "but" almost always points a contrast. Here we read, "But when he heard that Archelaus did reign in Judea in the room of his father Herod, he was afraid to go thither: notwithstanding, being warned of God in a dream, he turned aside into the parts of Galilee: And he came and dwelt in a city called Nazareth: that it might be fulfilled which was spoken by the prophets, He shall be called a Nazarene" (2:21-23). Nazareth was the most despised place in that despised province of Galilee, and thus we see how early the Messiah took the place of the despised One, again foreshadowing His rejection by the Jews—but mention of "Nazareth" *follows,* be it observed, mention of "the land of Israel."

Matthew 3 opens by bringing before us a most striking character: "In those days"—that is, while the Lord Jesus still dwelt in despised Nazareth of Galilee—"came John the Baptist, preaching in the wilderness of Judea." He was the predicted forerunner of Israel's Messiah. He was the one of whom Isaiah had said should prepare the way of the Lord, and this by preparing a people to receive Him by such time as He should appear to the public view. He came "in the spirit and power of Elijah" (Luke

WHY FOUR GOSPELS? 39

1:17), to do a work similar in character to that of the yet future mission of the Tishbite (Mal. 4:5, 6).

John addressed himself to the Covenant people, and restricted himself to the land of Judea. He preached not in Jerusalem but in the wilderness. The reason for this is obvious: God would not own the degenerate system of Judaism, but stationed His messenger *outside* all the religious circles of that. day. The "wilderness" but symbolized the barrenness and desolation of Israel's spiritual condition.

The *message* of John was simple and to the point —"Repent ye." It was a call for Israel to judge themselves. It was a word which demanded that the Jews take their proper place before God, confessing their sins. Only thus could a people be made ready for the Lord, the Messiah. The Call to Repentance was enforced by a timely warning—"Repent ye, *for* the Kingdom of Heaven is at hand." Observe, "Repent ye" not because "the Saviour is at hand," not because "God incarnate is now in your midst," and not because "A new Dispensation has dawned;" but, because "the Kingdom of Heaven" was "at hand." What would John's hearers understand by this expression? What meaning could those Jews attach to his words? Surely the Baptist did not employ language which, in the nature of the case, it was impossible for them to grasp. And yet we are asked to believe that John was here introducing Christianity! A wilder and more ridiculous theory it would be hard to imagine. If by the "Kingdom of Heaven" John signified the Christian dispensation, then he addressed those Jewish hearers in an unknown tongue. We say it with calm deliberation, that if John bade his auditors repent because the Christian dispensation was then being inaugurated, he *mocked* them, by employing a term which not only must have been entirely un-intelligible to them, but utterly mis-leading. To charge God's messenger with doing *that* is perilously near committing a sin which we shrink from naming.

What then, we ask again, would John's hearers understand him to mean when he said, "Repent ye, for the Kingdom of Heaven is at hand"? Addressing, as he was, a people who were familiar with the Old Testament Scriptures, they could place but one meaning upon his words, namely, that he was referring to the Kingdom spoken of again and again by their prophets—the *Messianic* Kingdom. That which should distinguish Messiah's Kingdom from all the kingdoms that have preceded it, is this: all the kingdoms of this world have been ruled over by Satan and his hosts, whereas, when Messiah's Kingdom is established, it shall be a rule of the Heavens over the earth.

The question has been raised as to why Israel *refused* the Kingdom on which their hearts were set. Did not the establishing of Messiah's Kingdom mean an end of the Roman dominion? and was not *that* the one thing they desired above all others? In reply to such questions several things must be insisted upon. In the first place, it is a *mistake* to say that Israel "refused" the Kingdom, for, in strict accuracy of language, the Kingdom was never "offered" to them—rather was the Kingdom heralded or proclaimed. The Kingdom was "at hand" because the Heir to David's throne was about to present Himself to them. In the second place, before the Kingdom could be set up, Israel must first *"Repent,"* but this, as is well known, is just what they, as a Nation, steadily refused to do. As we are expressly told in Luke 7:29, 30, "And all the people that heard him, and the publicans, justified God, being baptized with the baptism of John. But the Pharisees and lawyers *rejected* the counsel of God against themselves, being not baptized of him." In the third place, the reader will, perhaps, see our meaning clearer if we illustrate by an analogy: the world today is eagerly longing for the Golden Age. A millennium of peace and rest is the great desideratum among diplomats and politicians. But they want it *on their own terms*. They desire to bring it about by their own efforts. They have no desire for a Millennium brought about by the personal return to earth of the Lord Jesus Christ. Exactly so was it with Israel in the days of John the Baptist. True, they desired to be delivered from the Roman dominion. True, they wished to be freed for ever from the Gentile yoke. True, they longed for a millennium of undisturbed prosperity in a restored Palestine, *but they did not want it on GOD'S terms.*

The ministry of John the Baptist is referred to at greater or shorter length in each of the four Gospels, but Matthew is the only one who records this utterance "Repent ye, for the Kingdom of heaven is at hand." To ignore this fact is to fail in "rightly dividing the Word of truth." It is to lose sight of the characteristic distinctions which the Holy Spirit has been pleased to make in the four Gospels. It is to reduce those four independent delineations of Christ's person and ministry to a meaningless jumble. It is to lay bare the incompetency of a would-be-teacher of Scripture as one who is *not* a "scribe who is instructed unto the Kingdom of heaven" (Matt. 13:52).

John's baptism confirmed his preaching. He baptized "unto repentance," and in Jordan, the river of *death*. Those who were baptized "confessed their sins" (Mark 1:5), of which death was the just due, the "wages" earned. But Christian baptism is entirely different from this: *there*, we take not the place of those who deserve death, but of those who show forth the fact that they *have*, already, died with Christ.

It is beyond our present purpose to attempt a detailed exposition of this entire Gospel, rather shall we single out those features which are characteristic of and peculiar to this first Gospel. Accordingly, we may notice an expression found in 3:11, and which occurs nowhere else in the New Testament outside of the four Gospels, and this is the more remarkable because a *portion* of this very verse *is* quoted in the Acts. Speaking to the Pharisees and Sadducees who had "come to his baptism," but whom the Lord's forerunner quickly discerned were not in any condition to be baptized; who had been warned to flee from the wrath to come, and therefore were in urgent need of bringing forth "fruit meet for repentance" (in their case, humbling themselves before God, abandoning their lofty pretentions and self righteousness, and taking their place as genuine self-confessed sinners), and to whom John had said, "Think not to say within yourselves, We have Abraham to our father: for I say unto you, that God is able of these stones to raise up children unto (not *God*, be it noted, but) *Abraham*" (v. 9); to them John announced, "I indeed baptize you with water unto repentance: but he that cometh after me is mightier than I, whose shoes I am not worthy to bear: He shall baptize you with the Spirit and fire."

In Acts 1, where we behold the risen Lord in the

WHY FOUR GOSPELS? 43

midst of His disciples, we read, "And, being assembled together with them, commanded them that they should not depart from Jerusalem, but wait for the promise of the Father, which, saith He, ye have heard of Me. For John truly baptized with water: but ye shall be baptized with the Holy Spirit not many days hence" (vv. 4, 5). His forerunner had declared that Christ should baptize Israel with "the Holy Spirit *and fire,*" yet, here, the Lord speaks only of the disciples being baptized with the Holy Spirit. Why is this? Why did the Lord Jesus *omit* the words "and fire"? The simple answer is that in Scripture "fire" is, invariably, connected with *Divine judgment.* Thus, the reason is obvious why the Lord omits "and fire" from His utterance recorded in Acts 1. He was about to deal, not in judgment but, in grace! It is equally evident why the words "and fire" *are* recorded by Matthew, for his Gospel, deals, essentially with Dispensational relationships, and makes known much concerning Endtime conditions. God is yet to "baptize" recreant Israel "with fire," the reference being to the tribulation judgments, during the time of "Jacob's Trouble." Then will the winnowing fan be held by the hand of the rejected Messiah, and then "He will thoroughly purge His floor, and gather His wheat into the garner: but He will *burn up* the chaff with unquenchable fire" (Matt. 3:12). How manifestly do the words last quoted define for us the baptism of *"fire"!*

The silence of the risen Lord as to the "fire" when speaking to the disciples about "the baptism of the Spirit," has added force and significance when we find that *Mark's* Gospel gives the substance of what Matthew records of the Baptist's utterance, while *omit-*

ting the words "and fire"—"There cometh One mightier than I after me, the latchet of whose shoes I am not worthy to stoop down and unloose. I indeed have baptized you with water: but He shall baptize you with the Holy Spirit" (Mark 1:7, 8). Why is this? Because, as we have pointed out, "fire" is the well-known symbol of God's judgment (often displayed in *literal* fire), and Mark, who is presenting Christ as the Servant of Jehovah, was most obviously led of the Spirit *to leave out* the words "and fire," for as *Servant* He does not execute judgment. The words "and with fire" are found, though, in Luke, and this, again, is most significant. For, Luke is presenting Christ as "The Son of Man," and in John 5 we read, "And hath given Him authority to execute judgment also *because He is the Son of Man*" (v. 27). How strikingly, then, does the inclusion of the words "and fire" in Matthew and Luke, and their omission in Mark, bring out the *verbal* inspiration of Scripture, and the complete supervision of the Holy Spirit over the instruments He employed in the writing of God's Word!

The closing verses of Matt. 3 show us the Lord Jesus, in marvellous grace, taking His place with the believing remnant of Israel: "Then cometh Jesus from Galilee to Jordan unto John, to be baptized of him" (3:13). John was so startled that, at first, he *refused* to baptize Him—so little do the best of men enter into the meaning of the things of God—"But John forbad Him, saying, I have need to be baptized of Thee, and comest Thou to me?" (3:14). Observe once more, that Matthew is the only one of the Evangelists which mentions this shrinking of the Baptist from baptizing the Lord Jesus. Appropriately does it find a place here, for it brings out the

WHY FOUR GOSPELS? 45

royal dignity and majesty of Israel's Messiah. As to the meaning and significance of the Saviour's baptism we do not now enter at length, suffice it here to say that it revealed Christ as the One who had come down from heaven to act as the Substitute of His people, to die in their stead, and thus at the beginning of His public ministry He identifies Himself with those whom He represented, taking His place alongside of them in that which spoke of death. The descent of the Holy Spirit upon Him attested Him, indeed, as the true Messiah, the *Anointed* One (see Acts 10:38), and the audible testimony of the Father witnessed to His perfections, and fitness for the Work He was to do.

The first half of Matt. 4 records our Lord's Temptation, into which we do not now enter. The next thing we are told is, "Now when Jesus had heard that John was cast into prison, He departed into Galilee; And leaving Nazareth, He came and dwelt in Capernaum, which is upon the sea coast, in the borders of Zebulon and Naphtali" (4:12, 13), and this in order that a prophecy of Isaiah's might be fulfilled. And then we read, *"From that time Jesus began to preach, and to say, Repent: for the Kingdom of heaven is at hand"* (4:17). It would seem that the words "from that time" refer to the casting of the Baptist into prison. John's message had been, "Repent ye, for the Kingdom of heaven is at hand" (3:2), and now that His forerunner had been incarcerated, the Messiah Himself takes up identically the same message—the proclamation of the Kingdom. In keeping with this, we read, "And Jesus went about all Galilee teaching in their synagogues, and preaching the Gospel (not, be it noted, the "Gospel of the Grace of God"—Acts 20:24; nor "the Gospel of Peace"—Eph. 6:15; but "the Gospel") *of the Kingdom,* and healing all manner of sickness and all manner of disease among the people" (4:23).

Our Lord's miracles of healing were not simply exhibitions of power, or manifestations of mercy, they were also a supplement to His preaching and teaching, and their prime value was *evidential.* These miracles, which are frequently termed "signs," formed an essential part of Messiah's credentials. This is established, unequivocally, by what we read of in Matt. 11. When John the Baptist was cast into prison, his faith as to the Messiahship of Jesus wavered, and so he sent two of His disciples unto Him, asking, "Art Thou He that should come, or do we look for another?" (11:2). Notice, carefully, the Lord's reply, "Go and show John again those things which ye do *hear and see:* The blind receive their sight, and the lame walk, the lepers are cleansed, and the deaf hear, the dead are raised up, and the poor have the Gospel preached to them" (11:4, 5). Appeal was made to two things: His teaching and His miracles of healing. The two are linked together, again, in 9:35—"And Jesus went about all the cities and villages, teaching in their synagogues, and *preaching the Gospel of the Kingdom, and healing every sickness,* and every disease among the people." And, again, when the Lord sent forth the Twelve, "But go rather to the lost sheep of the House of Israel. And as ye go, *preach,* saying, The Kingdom of heaven is at hand. *Heal the sick,* raise the dead, cast out demons; freely ye have received, freely give" (10:6-8). Miracles of healing, then, were inseparately connected with *the Kingdom testimony.* They were among the most

WHY FOUR GOSPELS? 47

important of "The *Signs* of the times" concerning which the Messiah reproached the Pharisees and Sadducees for their failure to discern (see Matt. 16: 1-3). Similar miracles of healing shall be repeated when the Messiah returns to the earth, for we read in Is. 35:4-6, "Say to them that are of a fearful heart, Be strong, fear not: behold, your God will come with vengeance, even God with a recompense; He will come and save you (i. e., the godly Jewish remnant of the tribulation period). *Then the eyes of the blind shall be opened,* and the ears of the deaf shall be unstopped. Then shall the lame man leap as a hart, and the tongue of the dumb sing." It should be diligently observed that Matthew, once more, is the only one of the four Evangelists that makes mention of the Lord Jesus going forth and preaching "The Gospel *of the Kingdom,*" as he is the only one that informs us of the Twelve being sent out with the message to the lost sheep of the House of Israel, "The Kingdom of heaven is at hand." How significant this is! and how it indicates, again, the peculiarly *Jewish* character of these opening chapters of the New Testament!

As the result of these miracles of healing Messiah's fame went abroad throughout the length and breadth of the Land, and great multitudes followed Him. It is at this stage, we read, "And seeing the multitudes, He went up into a mountain: and when He was set, His disciples came unto Him: and He opened His mouth, and taught them" (5:1, 2). We are tempted to pause here, and enter into a detailed examination of this important, but much mis-understood portion of Scripture—the "Sermon on the Mount." But we must not depart from the central design of this book, hence a few words by way of summary is all we shall now attempt.

The first thing to be remarked is that "the Sermon on the Mount" recorded in Matt. 5 to 7 is peculiar to this first Gospel, no mention of it being made in the other three. This, together with the fact that in Matthew the "Sermon on the Mount" is found in the *first* section of the book, is sufficient to indicate its dispensational bearings. Secondly, the *place* from whence this "Sermon" was delivered affords another key to its scope. It was delivered from a *"mountain."* When the Saviour ascended the mount He was elevated above the common level, and did, in symbolic action, take His place upon the Throne. With Matt. 5:1 should be compared 17:1 —it was upon a *mountain* that the Messiah was "transfigured," and in that wondrous scene we behold a miniature and spectacular setting forth of "the Son of Man coming in His Kingdom" (see 16:28). Again, in 24:3, we find that it was upon a *mountain* that Christ gave that wondrous prophecy (recorded in 24 and 25) which describes the conditions which are to prevail just before the Kingdom of Christ is set up, and which goes on to tell of what shall transpire when He sits upon the Throne of His glory. With these passages should be compared two others in the Old Testament which clinch what we have just said above. In Zech. 14:4 we read, "And His feet shall stand in that day upon *the mount* of Olives," the reference being to the return of Christ to the earth to set up His Kingdom. Again, in Psalm 2 we read that God shall yet say, in reply to the concerted attempt of earth's rulers to prevent it,

"Yet have I set My *King* upon My holy *Hill of Zion*."*

The "Sermon on the Mount" sets forth *the Manifesto of the King*. It contains the "Constitution" of His Kingdom. It defines the character of those who shall enter into it. It tells of the experiences through which they pass while being fitted for that Kingdom. It enunciates the laws which are to govern their conduct. The *authority* of the King is evidenced by His "I say unto you," repeated no less than fourteen times in this "Sermon." The effect this had upon those who heard Him is apparent from the closing verses, "And it came to pass, when Jesus had ended these sayings, the people were astonished at His doctrine: for He taught them *as One having authority*, and not as the scribes" (7: 28, 29).

Another line of evidence which brings out Christ's *authority* (ever the most prominent characteristic in connection with a *King*), which is very pronounced in this Gospel, is seen in His command over the angels. One thing found in connection with kings is the many servants they have to wait upon them and do their bidding. So we find it here in connection with "the Son of David." In Matt. 13:41 we read, "The Son of man shall send forth His angels, and they shall gather out of His Kingdom all things that offend, and them which do iniquity." Observe that here these celestial servants

---

*In marked contrast from Matthew's "Sermon on the Mount" is Luke's "Sermon *in the Plain*"—6:17 etc. How significant and appropriate! Luke presents the Lord Jesus as "Son of Man," born in a manger, and entering into the sorrows and sufferings of men. How fitting, then, that *here* He should be heard speaking from "the Plain"—the common level, rather than from "the Mount," the place of eminence!

are termed not "the angels," but, specifically, *"His* angels," that is, Messiah's angels, and that they are sent forth in connection with "His. *Kingdom."* Again, in 24:30, 31 we read, "And they shall see the Son of man coming in the clouds of heaven with power and great glory (this, at His return to earth to establish His Kingdom). And He shall send *His angels* with a great sound of a trumpet, and they shall gather together His elect from the four winds, from one end of heaven to the other." And, again in 26:53, "Thinkest thou that I cannot now pray to (better, "ask") My Father, and He shall presently (immediately) give Me more than twelve legions of angels?" Matthew, be it particularly noted, *is the only one* that brings out this feature.

Still another line of evidence of the Kingly majesty of Christ should be pointed out. As it is well known, kings are honored by the homage paid them by their subjects. We need not be surprised, then, to find in this Gospel, which depicts the Saviour as "the Son of David," that Christ is frequently seen as the One before whom men prostrated themselves. Only once each in Mark, Luke, and John, do we read of Him *receiving worship,* but here in Matthew no less than *ten times!* See 2:2, 8, 11; 8:2; 9:18; 14:33; 15:25; 20:20; 28:9, 17.

Coming now to Matt. 10 (in 8 and 9 we have the Authentication of the King by the special miracles which He wrought), in the opening verses we have an incident which is recorded in each of the first three Gospels, namely, the selection and sending forth of the Twelve. But in Matthew's account there are several characteristic lines found nowhere else. For instance, only here do we learn that when the Lord sent them forth, He commanded them, say-

WHY FOUR GOSPELS? 51

ing, "Go not into the way of the Gentiles, and into any city of the Samaritans enter ye not: But go rather to the lost sheep of the House of Israel" (10:5, 6). Perfectly appropriate is this here, but it would have been altogether out of place in any of the others. Notice, also, that the Lord added, "And as ye go, preach, saying, The Kingdom of heaven is at hand." How the connection in which this expression is found *defines* for us its dispensational scope! It was only to "the lost sheep of the House *of Israel*" they were to say "The Kingdom of heaven is at hand"!

In Matt. 12 we have recorded the most remarkable miracle the Messiah performed before His break with Israel. It was the healing of a man possessed of a demon, and who, in addition, was both dumb and blind. Luke, also, records the same miracle, but in describing the effects this wonder had upon the people who witnessed it, Matthew mentions something which Luke omits, something which strikingly illustrates the special design of his Gospel. In the parallel passage in Luke 11:14 we read, "And He was casting out a demon, and it was dumb. And it came to pass, when the demon was gone out, the dumb spake; and the people wondered," and there the beloved physician stops. But Matthew says, "And all the people were amazed, and said, *Is not this the Son of David?*" (12:23). Thus we see, again, how that the bringing out of the *Kingship* of Christ is the particular object which Matthew, under the Holy Spirit, had before him.

In Matt. 13 we find the seven parables of the Kingdom (in its "mystery" form), the first of which is the well known parable of the Sower, the Seed, and the Soils. Both Mark and Luke also record it, but with characteristic differences of detail. We call attention to one point in Christ's interpretation of it. Mark reads, "The Sower soweth *the Word*" (4: 14). Luke says, "Now the parable is this: the Seed is *the Word of God*" (8:11). But Matthew, in harmony with his theme says, "Hear ye therefore the parable of the Sower. When anyone heareth *the Word of the Kingdom*" etc. (13:18, 19). This is but a minor point, but how it brings out the perfections of Holy Writ, down to the minutest detail! How evident it is that no mere man, or number of men, composed this Book of books! Well may we sing, "How firm a foundation, ye saints of the Lord, is laid for your faith in His excellent Word."

In Matt. 15 we have the well known incident of the Canaanitish woman coming to Christ on the behalf of her demon-distressed daughter. Mark also mentions the same, but omits several of the distinguishing features noted by Matthew. We quote first Mark's account, and then Matthew's, placing in italics the expressions which show forth the special design of his Gospel. "A certain woman whose young daughter had an unclean spirit, heard of Him, and came and fell at His feet. The woman was a Greek, a Syrophenician by nation; and she besought Him that He would cast forth the demon out of her daughter. But Jesus said unto her, Let the children first be filled: for it is not meet to take the children's bread, and to cast it unto the dogs. And she answered and said unto Him, Yes, Lord; yet the dogs under the table eat of the children's crumbs. And He said unto her, For this saying go thy way: the demon is gone out of thy daughter" (Mk. 7:25-29). "Behold, a woman of Canaan came out of the same coasts, and cried unto Him, saying, Have mer-

WHY FOUR GOSPELS? 53

cy on me, O Lord, *Thou Son of David:* my daughter is grievously vexed with a demon. *But He answered her not a word* (for, as a Gentile, she had no claim upon Him as the "Son of David"). And His disciples came and besought Him, saying, Send her away; for she crieth after us. But He answered and said, *I am not sent but unto the lost sheep of the House of Israel.* Then came she and worshipped Him, saying, Lord, help me. But He answered and said, It is not meet to take the children's bread, and to cast it to dogs. And she said, Truth, Lord; yet the dogs eat of the crumbs, which fall from their master's table. Then Jesus answered and said unto her, O woman great is thy faith: be it unto thee even as thou wilt" (Matt. 15:22-28).

In the opening verses of Matt. 16 we read of how the Pharisees and Sadducees came to Christ tempting Him, and desiring that He would show them a sign from heaven. Mark and Luke both refer to this, but neither of them record that part of our Lord's reply which is found here in verses 2 and 3— "He answered and said unto them, When it is evening, ye say, It will be fair weather: for the sky is red. And in the morning, It will be foul weather to day: for the sky is red and lowring. O ye hypocrites, ye can discern the face of the sky; but can ye not discern *the Signs of the Times?*" The "signs of the times" were the fulfillment of the Old Testament predictions concerning the Messiah. Every proof had been given to Israel that He was, indeed, the promised One. He had been born of a "virgin," in Bethlehem, the appointed place; a forerunner had prepared His way, exactly as Isaiah had foretold; and, in addition, there had been His mighty works, just as prophecy had fore-announced. But the Jews were blinded by their pride and self-righteousness. That Matthew alone makes mention of the Messiah's reference to these "Signs of the Times" is still another evidence of the distinctively *Jewish* character of his Gospel.

In Matt. 16:18 and 18:17 the "church" is twice referred to, and Matthew is the only one of the four Evangelists which makes any direct mention of it. This has puzzled many, but the explanation is quite simple. As previously pointed out, the great purpose of this first Gospel is to show how Christ presented Himself to the Jews, how they rejected Him as their Messiah, and what were the consequences of this, namely, the setting aside of Israel by God for a season, and His visiting the Gentiles in sovereign grace to take out of them a people for His name. Thus, are we here shown how that, and why, the Church has, in this dispensation, superseded the Jewish theocracy.

In Matt. 20 we have recorded the parable of the Householder, who went out and hired laborers for His vineyard, agreeing to pay them one penny for the day. Matthew is the only of the Evangelists that refers to this parable, and the pertinency of its place in his Gospel is clear on the surface. It brings out a characteristic of the *Kingship* of Christ. The parable tells of how, at the end of the day, when the workers came to receive their wages, there was complaining among them, because those hired at the eleventh hour received the same as those who had toiled all through the day—verily, there is nothing new under the sun, the dis-satisfaction of Labor being seen here in the first century! The Owner of the vineyard vindicated Himself by reminding the dis-contented workers that He paid to each what

WHY FOUR GOSPELS?

they had agreed to accept, and then inquired, "Is it not lawful for Me to do *what I will* with Mine own?" Thus did He, as *Sovereign,* insist on His rights to pay what *He* pleased, no one being wronged thereby.

In Matt. 22 we have the parable of the wedding-feast of the King's Son. A parable that is very similar to this one is found in Luke's Gospel, and while there are many points of resemblance between them, yet are there some striking variations. In Luke 14:16 we read, "Then said He unto him, *A certain man* made a great supper, and bade many." Whereas, in Matt. 22:2 we are told, "The Kingdom of heaven is like unto *a certain King,* which made a marriage for His Son." At the close of this parable in Matthew there is something which finds no parallel whatever in Luke. Here we read, "And when *the King* came in to see the guests, He saw there a guest which had not on a wedding garment: And He saith unto him, Friend, how camest thou in hither not having a wedding garment? And he was speechless. Then said *the King* to His servants, Bind him hand and foot, and take him away, and cast him into outer darkness: there shall be weeping, and gnashing of teeth" (22:11-13). How this brings out the *authority* of the King needs scarcely to be pointed out.

The whole of Matt. 25 is peculiar to this first Gospel. We cannot now dwell upon the contents of this interesting chapter, but would call attention to what is recorded in verses 31 to 46. That the contents of these verses is found nowhere else in the four Gospels, and its presence *here,* is another proof of the design and scope of Matthew's. These verses portray the Son of man seated upon the throne of His glory, and before Him are gathered all nations, these being divided into two classes, and stationed on His right and left hand, respectively. In addressing each class we read, "Then shall *the King* say" etc. (see verses 34, and 40).

There are a number of items concerning the Passion of the Lord Jesus recorded only by Matthew. In 26:59, 60 we read, "Now the chief priests, and elders, and all the council, sought false witnesses against Jesus, to put Him to death. But found none: yea, though many false witnesses came, yet found they none. At the last came *two* false witnesses"—two, because that was the minimun-number required by the law, in order that the truth might be established. It is interesting to note how frequently the two witnesses are found in Matthew. In 8:28 we read, "And when He was come to the other side into the country of the Gergesenes, there met Him *two* possessed with demons"—compare Mark 5:1, 2, where *only one* of these men is referred to. Again in 9:27 we read, "And when Jesus departed thence *two* blind men followed Him" etc.—compare Mark 10:46. In 11:2 we are told, "When John had heard in the prison the works of Christ, he sent *two* of his disciples." Finally, in 27:24 we find Pilate's testimony to the fact that Christ was a "just man," but in 27:19 we also read, "His wife sent unto him, saying, Have thou nothing to do with that *just man.*" And this, as well as the others cited above, is found *only in Matthew*. Again, in 26:63, 64 we find a characteristic word omitted from the other Gospels—"The high priest answered and said unto Him, I adjure thee by the living God, that Thou tell us whether Thou be the Christ, the Son of God. Jesus saith unto him, Thou hast said: nevertheless I say unto you, Hereafter shall ye see the Son of

WHY FOUR GOSPELS?

man *sitting on the right hand of power,* and coming in the clouds of heaven." Here only are we told that the guilty Jews cried, "His blood be on us, and on our children" (27:25). And again, Matthew is the only one that informs us of the enmity of Israel pursuing their Messiah even after His death—see 27:62-64.

The closing chapter of this Gospel is equally striking. No mention is made by Matthew of the *Ascension* of Christ. This, too, is in perfect accord with the theme and scope of this Gospel. The curtain falls here with the Messiah *still on earth,* for it is on earth, and not in heaven, that the Son of David shall yet reign in glory. Here only is recorded the Lord's word, "All power is given unto Me in heaven and in earth" (28:18)—for *"power"* is the outstanding mark of a king. Finally, the closing verses form a fitting conclusion, for they view Christ, on a "mountain," *commanding and commissioning* His servants to go forth and disciple the nations, ending with the comforting assurance, "Lo, I am with you alway, even unto the end of the Age."

THE GOSPEL OF MARK.

THE GOSPEL OF MARK.

MARK'S Gospel differs widely from Matthew's, both in character and scope. The contrasts between them are marked and many. Matthew has twenty-eight chapters, Mark but sixteen. Matthew abounds in parables, Mark records but few. Matthew portrays Christ as the Son of David, Mark delineates Him as the humble but perfect Servant of Jehovah. Matthew is designed particularly (not exclusively) for the Jew, whereas Mark is specially appropriate for Christian workers. Matthew sets forth the Kingly dignity and authority of Christ, Mark views Him in His lowliness and meekness. Matthew depicts Him as testing Israel, Mark shows Him ministering to the Chosen People. This is one reason why, no doubt, that Mark's Gospel is the second book in the New Testament—like Matthew's, it views Him in connection with the Old Testament people of God. Luke's Gospel, has a wider scope, looking at Christ in relation to the human race. While in John, He is shown to be the Son of God, spiritually related to the household of faith. In turning now to look at the contents of this second Gospel in some detail, we would notice,

I. THINGS OMITTED FROM MARK'S GOSPEL.

1. Just as the skill of a master artist is discovered in the objects which he leaves out of his picture (the amateur crowding in everything on to the canvass for which he can find room), so the discerning eye at once detects the handiwork of the Holy Spirit in the various things which are included and omitted from different parts of the Word. Notably is this the case with Mark's Gospel. Here we find no Genealogy at the commencement, as in Matthew; the miraculous Conception is omitted, and there is no mention made of His Birth. Fancy a whole Gospel written and yet no reference to the Saviour's birth in it! At first glance this is puzzling, but a little reflection assures one of the Divine wisdom which directed Mark to say nothing about it. Once we see what is the special design of each separate Gospel, we are the better enabled to appreciate their individual perfections. The *birth* of Christ did not fall within the compass of this second Gospel, nor did the record of His genealogy. Mark is presenting Christ as the Servant of Jehovah, and in connection with a *servant* a genealogy or particulars of birth are scarcely points of interest or importance. But how this demonstrates the Divine Authorship of the books of the Bible! Suppose the Genealogy had been omitted by Matthew, and inserted by Mark, then, the unity of each Gospel would be destroyed. But just as the Creator placed each organ of the body in the wisest possible place, so the Holy Spirit guided in the placing of each book in the Bible (each member in this Living Organism), and each detail of each book. For the same reason as the Genealogy is omitted, nothing is said by Mark of the visit of the wise men, for a "servant" is not one that receives homage! Mark also passes over what Luke tells us of Christ as a boy of twelve in the temple of Jerusalem, and His subsequent return to Nazareth, where He continued in subjection to His parents, for, while these are points of interest in connection with His humanity, they were irrelevent to a setting forth of His Servanthood.

WHY FOUR GOSPELS?

2. In Mark's Gospel we find no Sermon on the Mount. Matthew devotes three whole chapters to it, but Mark records it not, though some of its teachings are found in other connections in this second Gospel. Why, then, we may ask, is this important utterance of Christ omitted by Mark? The answer must be sought in the character and design of the "Sermon." As we have pointed out, the Sermon on the Mount contains the King's Manifesto. It sets forth the laws of His Kingdom, and describes the character of those who are to be its subjects. But Mark is presenting Christ as the perfect Workman of God, and a *servant* has no "Kingdom," and frames no "laws." Hence the appropriateness of the "Sermon" in Matthew, and the Divine wisdom in its exclusion from Mark.

3. Mark records fewer Parables than Matthew. In Mark there are but four all told, whereas in Matthew there are at least fourteen. Mark says nothing about the Householder hiring laborers for His vineyard, claiming the right to do as He wills with that which is His own; for, as God's Servant, He is seen in the place of the Laborer, instead of in the position where He hires others. Mark omits all reference to the parable of the Marriage of the King's Son, at the close of which He is seen giving orders for the man without the wedding-garment to be bound and cast into the outer darkness—such is not the prerogative of a Servant. All reference to the parable of the Talents is omitted by Mark, for as God's Servant He neither gives talents nor rewards for the use of them. Each of these parables, and many others all found in Matthew, are excluded by Mark, and their omission only serves to bring out the minute perfections of each Gospel.

64   WHY FOUR GOSPELS?

4. In Mark nothing whatever is said of Christ's command over angels, and His right to send them forth to do His bidding; instead we find here "the angels ministered *unto* Him" (1:13).

5. Here there is no arraignment of Israel, and no sentence is passed upon Jerusalem as in the other Gospels. Again, in Matt. 23 the "Son of David" utters a most solemn sevenfold "Woe"—"Woe unto you scribes and Pharisees, hypocrites," "Woe unto you, ye blind guides" etc., He says there: but not a word of this is found in Mark. The reason for this is obvious. It is not the part of the *Servant* to pass judgment on others, but "to be gentle unto all, apt to teach, patient" (2 Tim. 2:24). We have another striking illustration of this same characteristic in connection with our Lord cleansing the Temple. In Matt. 21:12 we read, "And Jesus went into the temple of God, and cast out all them that sold and bought in the temple, and overthrew the tables of the moneychangers, and the seats of them that sold doves," and immediately following this we are told, "And He left them, and went out of the city into Bethany: and He lodged there" (21:17). But in Mark it is simply said, "And Jesus entered into Jerusalem, and into the temple: and when He had looked round about upon all things, and now the eventide was come, He went out unto Bethany with the twelve" (11:11). Mark is clearly writing of the same incident. He refers to the Lord entering the temple, but says nothing about Him casting out those who bought and sold there, nor of Him overthrowing the tables. How striking is this omission. As the Messiah and King it was fitting that He should cleanse the defiled Temple, but in His character of Servant it would have been incongruous!

WHY FOUR GOSPELS?

6. The omission of so many of the Divine titles from this second Gospel is most significant. In Mark, He is never owned as "King" save in derision. In Mark, we do not read, as in Matthew, "They shall call His name Immanuel, which being interpreted is, God with us," and only once is He here termed "the Son of David." It is very striking to observe how the Holy Spirit has avoided this in the second Gospel. In connection with the "Triumphant Entry into Jerusalem," when recording the acclamations of the people, Matthew says, "And the multitudes that went before, and that followed, cried, saying, Hosanna to the Son of David: Blessed is He that cometh in the name of the Lord; Hosanna in the highest" (21:9). But in Mark's account we read, "And they that went before, and they that followed, cried, saying, Hosanna: Blessed is He that cometh in the name of the Lord: Blessed be the Kingdom of our father David, that cometh in the name of the Lord: Hosanna in the highest" (11:9, 10). Thus it will be seen that the Servant of God was not hailed here as "the Son of David." Side by side with this, should be placed the words used by our Lord when announcing, a week beforehand, His "transfiguration." In Matthew's account, we read that He told His disciples, "Verily I say unto you, There be some standing here, which shall not taste of death, till they see the Son of Man coming in His Kingdom." But, here in Mark, we are told that He said to the disciples, "Verily I say unto you, That there be some of them that stand here, which shall not taste of death, till they have seen the Kingdom of God come with power" (9:1). How significant this is! Here it is simply the "Kingdom *of God"* that is spoken of, instead of Christ's *own* Kingdom!

But that which is most noteworthy here in connection with the titles of Christ, is the fact that He is so frequently addressed as "Master," when, in the parallel passages in the other Gospels, He is owned as "Lord." For example: in Matt. 8:25 we read, "And His disciples came to Him, and awoke Him, saying, *Lord*, save us; we perish;" but in Mark, "And they awake Him, and say unto Him, *Master*, carest Thou not that we perish?" (4:38). Following the announcement of His coming death, Matthew tells us, "Then Peter took Him, and began to rebuke Him, saying, Be it far from Thee, Lord: this shall not be unto Thee" (16:22). But in Mark it reads, "And Peter took Him, and began to rebuke Him" (8:32), and there it stops. On the Mount of Transfiguration, Peter said, *"Lord,* it is good for us to be here" (17:4); but Mark says, "And Peter answered and said to Jesus, *Master,* it is good for us to be here" (9:5). When the Saviour announced that one of the Twelve would betray Him, Matthew tells us, "And they were exceeding sorrowful, and began every one of them to say unto Him, *Lord,* is it I?" (26:22); but Mark tells us, "And they began to be sorrowful, and to say unto Him, one by one, "Is it I?" (14:19). These are but a few of the examples which might be adduced, but sufficient have been given to bring out this striking and most appropriate feature of Mark's Gospel.

7. It is deeply interesting and instructive to note the various circumstances and events connected with our Lord's sufferings which are omitted from Mark. Here, as He entered the awful darkness of Gethsemane, He says to the three disciples, "Tarry ye here,

and watch" (14:34), not "watch *with Me,*" as in Matthew, for as the Servant He turns only to God for comfort; and here, nothing is said at the close, of an angel from Heaven appearing and "strengthening" Him, for as Servant He draws strength from God alone. No mention is made by Mark of Pilate's "I find no fault in Him," nor are we told of Pilate's wife counselling her husband to have nothing to do with "this Just Man," nor do we read here of Judas returning to the priests, and saying, "I have betrayed innocent blood;" all of these are omitted by Mark, for the Servant must look to God alone for vindication. Nothing is said in Mark of the women following Christ as He was led to the place of execution, "bewailing and lamenting Him" (Luke 23: 27), for sometimes the suffering Servant of God is denied the sympathy of others. The words of the dying thief, "Lord, remember me when Thou comest into Thy Kingdom" are here omitted, for in this Gospel, Christ is neither presented as "Lord" nor as One having a "Kingdom." The Saviour's triumphant cry from the Cross, "It is finished" is also omitted. At first sight this seems strange, but a little reflection will discover the Divine wisdom for its exclusion. It is not for the *Servant* to say when his work is finished—that is for *God* to decide! We pass on now to notice

II. THINGS WHICH ARE CHARACTERISTIC OF MARK.

1. Mark's Gospel opens in a manner quite different from the others. In Matthew, Luke and John, there is what may be termed a lengthy Introduction, but in Mark it is quite otherwise. Matthew records Christ's genealogy, His birth, the visit and homage of the wise men, the flight into

Egypt, and subsequent return and sojourn in Nazareth; describes at length both His baptism and temptation, and not till we reach the end of the fourth chapter do we arrive at His public ministry. Luke opens with some interesting details concerning the parentage of John the Baptist, describes at length the interview between the angel and the Saviour's mother previous to His birth, records her beautiful Song, tells of the angelic visitation to the Bethlehem shepherds at Christ's birth, pictures the presentation of the Child in the temple, and refers to many other things; and not until we reach the fourth chapter do we come to the public ministry of the Redeemer. So, too, in John. There is first a lengthy Prologue, in which is set forth the Divine glories of the One who became flesh; then follows the testimony of His forerunner to the Divine dignity of the One he had come to herald; then we have described a visit to John of a delegation sent from Jerusalem to inquire as to who he was; finally, there is the witness of the Baptist to Christ as the Lamb of God: and all this before we here read of Him calling His first disciples. But how entirely different is the opening of the second Gospel. Here there is but a brief notice of the Baptist and his testimony, a few words concerning Christ's baptism and His temptation, and then in the fourteenth verse of the *first* chapter we read, "Now after that John was put in prison, Jesus came into Galilee, preaching the gospel of the Kingdom of God." The first thirty years of His life here on earth are passed over in silence, and Mark at once introduces Christ at the beginning of His public ministry. *Mark presents Christ actually serving.*

2. The opening verse of Mark is very striking:

WHY FOUR GOSPELS?

"The beginning of the Gospel of Jesus Christ, the Son of God." Observe, it is not here "the Gospel *of the Kingdom*" (as in Matthew), but "the Gospel of Jesus Christ." How significant that it is added "the Gospel of Jesus Christ, *the Son of God*." Thus has the Holy Spirit guarded His Divine glory in the very place where His lowliness as the "Servant" is set forth. It is also to be remarked that this word "Gospel" is found much more frequently in Mark than in any of the other Gospels. The term "Gospel" occurs twelve times in all in Matthew, Mark, Luke, and John, and no less than eight of these are found in Mark, so that the word "Gospel" is found twice as often in Mark as in the other three added together! The reason for this is obvious: as the Servant of Jehovah, the Lord Jesus was the Bearer of good news, the Herald of glad tidings! What a lesson to be taken to heart by all of the servants of God to-day!

3. Another characteristic term which occurs with even greater frequency in this second Gospel is the Greek word "Eutheos," which is variously translated "forthwith, straightway, immediately" etc. Notice a few of the occurrences of this word in the first chapter alone: "And *straightway* coming up out of the water, He saw the heavens opened, and the Spirit like a dove descending upon Him" (v. 10). "And *immediately* the Spirit driveth Him into the wilderness" (v. 12). "And when He had gone a little farther thence, He saw James the son of Zebedee, and John his brother, who also were in the ship mending their nets, And *straightway* He called them" (vv. 19, 20). "And they went into Capernaum; and *straightway* on the sabbath day He entered into the synagogue, and taught" (v. 21).

"And *forthwith* when they were come out of the synagogue, they entered into the house of Simon" (v. 29). "And He came and took her by the hand, and lifted her up, and *immediately* the fever left her" (v. 31). "And He straightly charged him, and *forthwith* sent him away" (v. 43). In all, this word is found no less than forty times in Mark's Gospel. It is a most suggestive and expressive term, bringing out the perfections of God's Servant by showing us *how* He served. There was no tardiness about Christ's service, but "straightway" He was ever about His "Father's business." There was no delay, but "forthwith" He performed the work given Him to do. This word tells of the *promptitude* of His service and the *urgency* of His mission. There was no holding back, no reluctance, no slackness, but a blessed "immediateness" about all His work. Well may we learn from this perfect example which He has left us.

4. The way in which so many of the chapters open in this second Gospel is worthy of our close attention. Turn to the first verse of chapter 2, *"And again He entered into Capernaum after some days."* Again, the first verse of chapter 3, *"And He entered again into the synagogue."* So in 4:1, *"And He began again to teach by the seaside."* So in 5:1, *"And they came over unto the other side of the sea."* This is seemingly a trivial point, and yet, how unique! It is now more than ten years since the writer first observed this feature of Mark's Gospel, and since then, many hundreds of books, of various sorts, have been read by him, but never once has he seen a single book of human authorship which had in it one chapter that commenced with the word "And." Test this, reader, by your own library.

WHY FOUR GOSPELS? 71

Yet here in Mark's Gospel no less than twelve of its chapters begin with "And"!

"And," as we know, is a conjunction joining together two other parts of speech; it is that which links two or more things together. The service of Christ, then, was characterized by that which "And" signifies. In other words, *His* service was one complete and perfect whole, *with no breaks in it*. Ah, how *unlike* ours! Yours and mine is so disjointed.

We serve God for a time, and then there comes a slackening up, a pause, a break, which is followed by a period of inactivity, before we begin again. But not so with Christ. His service was a series of perfect acts, fitly joined together, without a break or blemish. "And," then, as characterizing the service of Christ, tells of *ceaseless* activity. It speaks of the *continuity* of His labors. It shows us how *He* was "instant in season and out of season." It reveals how He never grew weary of well doing. May God's grace cause the "And" to have a more prominent place in our service for Him.

5. In the former section we have pointed out how that Mark records fewer parables than Matthew, and we may add, fewer than Luke too. But, on the other hand, Mark describes more miracles. This, also, is in keeping with the design and scope of this second Gospel. Parables contained our Lord's teachings, whereas the miracles were a part of His active ministry. Service consists more of deeds than teaching, doing rather than speaking. How often *our* service is more with our lips than our hands. We are big talkers and little doers!

Mark records just four parables, and it is a most significant thing that each of them has to do, directly, with service. The first is the parable of the

Sower, and this views the Saviour as going forth with the Word (4:3-20). The second parable is that of the Seed cast into the ground, which sprang up and grew, and brought forth first the blade, then the ear, after that the full corn in the ear, and finally was harvested (4:26-29). The third parable is that of the Mustard-seed (4:30-32). The fourth is that of the Wicked Husbandmen who mistreated the Owner's servants, and ended by killing His well-beloved Son (12:1-9). Thus it will be seen, that each has to do with ministry or service: the first three with sowing Seed, and the last with the Servant going forth "that He might receive of the husbandman *of the fruit* of the vineyard."

6. In Mark's Gospel, the *hand* of Christ is frequently mentioned, and this is peculiarly appropriate in the Gospel which treats of His service. It might well be termed, *the Ministry of the Hand*. How prominent this feature is here may be seen by consulting the following passages. "And He came and *took her by the hand,* and lifted her up; and immediately the fever left her" (1:31). "And Jesus, moved with compassion, *put forth His hand, and touched him,* and saith unto him, I will; be thou clean" (1:41). "And He *took the damsel by the hand,* and said unto her, Talitha cumi: which is, being interpreted, Damsel, I say unto thee, arise" (5:41). "And they bring unto Him one that was deaf, and had an impediment in his speech; and they beseech Him *to put His hand upon him*" (7:32). How beautiful is this. Divinely enlightened, these people had learned of the tenderness and virtue of *His* hand. Again we read, "And He cometh to Bethsaida; and they bring a blind man unto Him, and besought Him *to touch him*" (8:22).

They, too, had discovered the blessedness and power of His touch. "And *He took the blind man by the hand,* and led him out of the town. * * After that *He put His hands again upon his eyes,* and made him look up: and he was restored, and saw every man clearly" (8:23, 25). Once more we read, "But Jesus *took him by the hand,* and lifted him up; and he arose" (9:27). How blessed for every believer to know that he is safely held in that same blessed Hand (John 10:28).

7. The Holy Spirit has also called special attention in this Gospel to the *eyes* of the perfect Servant. "And when He had *looked* round about on them with anger, being grieved for the hardness of their hearts" (3:5). How those Holy eyes must have flashed upon those who would condemn Him for healing on the Sabbath day the man with the withered hand! "And He *looked* round about on them which sat about Him, and said, Behold My mother and My brethren! For whosoever shall do the will of God, the same is My brother, and My sister, and My mother" (3:34, 35). This time the Saviour's eyes were turned upon His disciples, and what love must have appeared in them as He turned and beheld those who had forsaken all to follow Him! "But when He had turned about and *looked* on His disciples, He rebuked Peter, saying, Get thee behind Me, Satan" (8:33). What a touch in the picture is this—before He rebuked Peter, He, first, turned, and "looked" on His disciples! Concerning the rich young ruler who came to Him, we read here (and here only)," Then Jesus *beholding* him, loved him" (10:21). What Divine pity and compassion must have shone in His eyes at that moment! So again in 11:11 we read, "And Jesus entered into Je-

rusalem, and into the temple, and when He had *looked* round upon all things, and now the eventide was come, He went out into Bethany with the twelve." How those eyes must have blazed with righteous indignation, as He beheld the desecration of the Father's house! These passages which mention the Saviour "looking" and "beholding", tell us of His thoughtfulness, His attention to detail, His thoroughness. Next we will notice,

III. THE MANNER IN WHICH CHRIST SERVED.

In order to discover the manner in which Christ served, we must examine closely the details of what the Holy Spirit has recorded here for our learning and profit, and for the benefit of our readers we shall classify those under suitable headings.

1. Christ served with marked Unostentation.

"And Simon and they that were with him followed after Him. And when they had found Him, they said unto Him, *All men seek for Thee*. And He said unto them, *Let us go* into the next towns, that I may preach there also: for therefore came I forth" (Mark 1:36-38). This incident occurred near the beginning of our Lord's public ministry. He had wrought some mighty works, many of the sick had been healed, and His fame had gone abroad. In consequence, great throngs of people sought for Him. He was, for a brief season, the popular Idol of the hour. But what was His response? Instead of remaining where He was to receive the plaudits of a fickle crowd, He moves away to preach in other towns. How unlike many of us to day! When we are well received, when we become the center of an admiring crowd, *our* desire is to *remain* there. Such a reception is pleasing to the flesh; it panders to our pride. We like to boast of the crowds that attend our ministry. But the perfect Servant of God never courted popularity, *He shunned it!* And when His disciples came and told Him—no doubt with pleasurable pride—"All men seek for Thee," His immediate response was, "Let us *go*"*!*

At the close of Mark 1 we read of a leper being cleansed by the great Physician, and, dismissing him, He said, *"See thou say nothing to any man:* but go thy way, shew thyself to the priest, and offer for thy cleansing those things which Moses commanded, for a testimony unto them." How utterly unlike many of His servants to day, who spare no pains or expense to *advertise themselves!* How entirely different we are from the One who said, "I receive not honor *from men*" (John 5:41)! No; *He* ever wrought with an eye *single* to God's glory. Notice, farther, how this comes out again in the sequel to the above miracle. The healed leper heeded not the admonition of his Benefactor, instead, we read, "But he went out, and began to publish it much, and to blaze abroad the matter." How gratifying this would have been to most of us! But not so with Him who sought only the Father's glory. Instead of following the man who had been healed, to become the Object of the admiring gaze and flattering remarks of the leper's friends and neighbors, we read, that "Jesus could no more openly enter into the city, *but was without in desert places"!* Are we not to learn from this, that when people begin to "blaze abroad" what God has wrought through us, it is time for us to move on, lest we receive the honor and glory which is due Him alone!

In full harmony with what has just been before

us in the closing verses of Mark 1, we read in the first verses of the next chapter, "And again He entered into Capernaum, after some days, and it was noised that *He was in the house,*" for, evidently, the healed leper belonged to that highly favored town. Hence it was that we here find Him seeking the privacy and quietude of the "house." So again in 3:19 we read, "And they (Christ and the apostles) *went into an house.*" His reason for doing this, here, was to escape from the crowd, as is evident from the words which immediately follow, "And the multitude cometh together again." Again in 7:17 we are told, "And when He was *entered into the house* from the people." His life was not lived before the footlights, but quietly and unobtrusively He went about doing the Father's will. What a word is this —"And when He was entered into the house *from the people*"! And how different from some of His servants today, whose one great aim seems to be the *seeking* of the patronage of "the people," and the soliciting of their favors! So, again in 9:28 we read, "And when *He was come into the house,* His disciples asked Him privately, Why could not we cast him out?" (9:28). And once more in 9:33, we read "And He came to Capernaum: and *being in the house* He asked them, What was it that ye disputed among yourselves by the way?" Mark, we may add, is the only one of the four Evangelists that makes this repeated reference to "the house." It is just one of the smaller lines in the picture that serves to bring out the Unostentation of the perfect Servant.

In the closing verses of Mark 7 we have recorded the miracle of Christ restoring one that was deaf and had an impediment in his speech. And in chapter

WHY FOUR GOSPELS?

eight is recorded the healing of the blind man, who, at the first touch of the Lord's hands saw men as trees walking, but who, at the second touch "saw every man clearly." Mark is the only one that records either of these miracles. One reason for their inclusion here, is seen in a feature that is common to them both. In 7:36 we are told, "And He charged them *that they should tell no man:* but the more He charged them, so much the more a great deal they published it." Concerning the latter we read, "And He sent him away to his house, saying, *Neither go into the town, nor tell it to any in the town*" (8:26). What a lesson for all of us: perfect service is rendered to God alone, and often is unseen, unappreciated, unthanked by man. The Servant of Jehovah threw a veil over His gracious acts.

2. *Christ served with great Tenderness.*

This comes out so often in this second Gospel. We single out four examples, and the better to appreciate them, we quote first the parallel references in the other Gospels, before noticing Mark's account. "And Simon's wife's mother was taken with a great fever; and they besought Him for her. And He stood over her, and rebuked the fever; and it left her; and immediately she arose and ministered unto them" (Luke 4:38, 39). "But Simon's wife's mother lay sick of a fever, and anon they tell Him of her. And He came *and took her by the hand, and lifted her up;* and immediately the fever left her, and she ministered unto them" (Mk. 1:30, 31). What a beautiful line in the picture is this! How it shows us that Christ's service was no mere perfunctory one, performed with mechanical indifference, but that He came near to those to whom He ministered and entered, sympathetically, into their condition.

In Luke 9 we read of the father who sought out the Lord Jesus on behalf of his demon-possessed son, and in healing him we read, "And Jesus rebuked the unclean spirit, and healed the child, and delivered him again to his father" (9:42). But Mark brings into his picture a characteristic line which Luke omitted, "But Jesus *took him by the hand, and lifted him up,* and he arose" (9:27). There was no aloofness about the perfect Servant. How this rebukes the assumed self-superiority of those who think it beneath their dignity to shake hands with those to whom they have ministered the Word! To take some people "by the hand" is to get nearer their hearts. Let us seek to serve as Christ did.

In Matt. 18:2 we read, "And Jesus called a little child unto Him, and set him in the midst of them." But on another occasion, Mark tells us, "And He took a child, and set him in the midst of them: *and when He had taken him in His arms,* He said unto them" (9:36). Again, in Matt. 19:13-15 we are told, "Then were there brought unto Him little children, that He should put His hands on them, and pray: and the disciples rebuked them. But Jesus said, Suffer little children, and forbid them not, to come unto Me, for of such is the kingdom of heaven. And He laid His hands on them, and departed thence." But once more we may observe how that Mark adds a line all his own, "And they brought young children to Him, that He should touch them: and His disciples rebuked those that brought them. But when Jesus saw it, He was much displeased, and said unto them, Suffer the little children to come unto Me, and forbid them not: for of such is the kingdom of God. Verily I say unto you, Whosoever shall not receive the kingdom of God as a little child, he shall not enter therein. *And He took them up in His arms,* put His hands upon them, and blessed them" (10:13-16). What *tenderness* do these acts display! And what an example He has left us!

3. Christ served encountering great Opposition.

Here we shall take a rapid review of Mark's reference to this feature of his theme, instead of commenting on each passage, though a remark here and there will, perhaps, not be out of place.

"But there were certain of the scribes sitting there, and *reasoning in their hearts* (there are usually a few such in most congregations), Why does this man *thus speak blasphemies?"* (2:6, 7). "And when the scribes and Pharisees saw Him eat with publicans and sinners, they said unto His disciples, *How is it* that He eateth and drinketh with publicans and sinners?" (2:16). "And the Pharisees said unto Him, behold, *why* do they on the sabbath day that which is not lawful?" (2:24). The servant of God must expect to be mis-understood and encounter criticism and opposition. "And *they watched Him* whether He would heal him on the sabbath day" (3:2). And the servant of God is still watched by unfriendly eyes! "And the Pharisees went forth, and straightway took counsel with the Herodians against Him, how they might *destroy Him"* (3:6). Every faction of the people was "against" Him. "And the scribes which came down from Jerusalem said, He *hath Beelzebub,* and by the prince of the demons casteth He out demons" (3:22). The servant may expect to be called hard names. "And they began to pray Him *to depart* out of their coasts" (5:17). Christ was not wanted. His testimony condemned His hearers. So will it be now with every servant of God that is *faithful*. "And they *laughed Him to scorn*" (5:40). To be sneered and jeered at, then, is nothing new: sufficient for the disciple to suffer what his Master did before him. "And they were *offended* at Him" (6:3). The Christ of God did not suit everybody; far from it. But let us see to it that we give none other occasion for "offence" than He did! "And He could *there* do no mighty work, save that He laid His hands upon *a few* sick folk, and healed them" (6:5). The servant of God will come to some places which are unfavorable for effective ministry, and where the unbelief of the profest people of the Lord will hinder the Spirit of God." Then came together unto Him the Pharisees, and certain of the scribes, which came from Jerusalem. And when they saw some of His disciples eat bread with defiled, that is to say, with unwashen hands, *they found fault*" (7:1, 2). Nevertheless, the Lord Jesus declined to respect *their* "traditions," refusing to allow His disciples to be brought into bondage thus. Well for God's servants now if they disregard the "touch not, taste not, handle not" of *men,* yet must they be prepared to be "found fault" with as the result. "And the Pharisees came forth, and began to question with Him, seeking of Him a sign from heaven, *tempting Him*" (8:11). So, too, will the emissaries of the Enemy seek now to entangle and ensnare the servants of God. Compare Mark 10:2. "And the scribes and chief priests heard it, and sought how they might destroy Him: for they feared Him, *because all the people was astonished at His doctrine*" (11:18). They were jealous of His influence. And human nature has not changed since then! "And they come again to Jerusalem: and as He was walking in the temple, there came to Him the chief priests and the scribes, and the elders. And say unto Him, *By what authority* doest Thou these things? and *who* gave Thee this authority?" (11: 27, 28). How history repeats itself! From what College have you graduated? and in which Seminary were you trained? are the modern form of this query. "And they sent unto Him certain of the Pharisees, and of the Herodians, *to catch Him in His words*" (12:13). And some of their descendants still survive, and woe be to the man who fails to pronounce *their* shiboleths! What a list this is! and we have by no means exhausted it; see further 12:18; 12:28; 14:1 etc. All the way through, the perfect Servant of God was dogged by His enemies; at every step He encountered opposition and persecution in some form. And these things are all recorded for our instruction. The Enemy is not dead. God's servants today are called to tread a similar path.

4. Christ Served with much Self-Sacrifice.

"And the multitude cometh together again, so that *they could not so much as eat bread*" (3:20). So thoroughly was He at the disposal of others. How completely did He know what it was to spend and be spent!

"And the same day, *when the even was come*, He saith unto them, Let us pass over unto the other side. And when *they* had sent away the multitude, they *took* Him, *even as He was* into the ship" (4: 35, 36). How touching is this! A study of the context, with the parallel passages in the other Gospel, shows this evening here was the close of a busy and crowded day. From early morn till sunset, the Master had been ministering to others, and now He is so weary and worn from His labors He had to be "taken"—led and lifted—into the ship! "Even as He was"—how much do these words cover? Ah, Christian worker, next time you come to the close of a full day of service for God, and your mind is tired and your nerves are quivering, remember that thy Lord, before thee, knew what it was to lay down (see 4:38) so tired that even the storm awoke Him not!

"And He said unto them, Come ye yourselves apart into a desert place, and rest a while: for there were many coming and going, and *they had NO leisure so much as to eat*" (6:31). That is how the perfect Workman of God served. Ever attent in being about His Father's business: no rest, no leisure, at times so thronged that He went without His meals.

Christ's service *cost Him something*. Note how this comes out in the next quotations. "And when He had looked round about on them with anger, *being grieved* for the hardness of their hearts" (3:5). He was no frigid Stoic. "And looking up to heaven *He sighed*, and saith unto him, Ephphatha, that is, Be opened" (7:34). Christ's service was not rendered formally and perfunctarily; but He entered, sympathetically, into the condition of the sufferer. "And *He sighed deeply* in His spirit, and saith, Why doth this generation seek after a sign?" (8:12). Thus did He take to heart the sad unbelief of those to whom He ministered. He suffered inwardly as well as outwardly.

"And the multitude cometh together again, so that they could not so much as eat bread. And *when*

His friends heard of it, they went out to lay hold on Him: *for they said, He is beside Himself"* (3: 20, 21). So incapable were they of entering into the thoughts of God. They sought to check Him in the accomplishing of God's will. Their purpose was well meant, no doubt, but it was a zeal "without knowledge." What a warning· is this for all of God's servants. Watch out for well intentioned "friends" who, lacking in discernment, may seek to hinder the one who is completely yielded to God, and who, like the apostle Paul, "counts not his life dear unto himself" (Acts 20:24).

5. Christ Served in an Orderly manner.

This comes out, in an incidental way, in several statements which are found only in Mark. We single out but two. In 6:7 we read, "And He called unto Him the twelve, and began to send them forth *by two and two."* Again; when about to feed the hungering multitude, we are here told, "And He commanded them to make them all sit down by companies upon the green grass. And they sat down *in ranks, by hundreds, and by fifties"* (6:39, 40). What attention to details was this! And how it rebukes much of our slipshod work! If Scripture enjoins, *"Whatsoever* thine hand findeth to do, do it with thy might," then, surely our service for God calls for our most careful and prayerful attention! God is never the author of "confusion," as Christ's example here plainly shows.

6. Christ's Service was prompted by Love.

"And Jesus, *moved with compassion,* put forth His hand, and touched him (the leper), and said unto him, I will; be thou clean" (1:41). "And Jesus, when He came out, saw much people, and was *moved with compassion* toward them, because they were as sheep not having a shepherd; and He began to teach them many things" (6:34). *"I have compassion on the multitude,* because they have now been with Me three days, and have nothing to eat" (8:1). Mark is the only one of the Evangelists that brings this lovely and touching line into the picture. And O how it rebukes the writer for his *hardness* of heart, and cold indifference to the perishing all around! How little real "compassion" one finds today! "Then Jesus beholding him (the rich young man) *loved him"* (Mark 10:21). Mark is the only one who tells us this, as though to show that without "love" service is barren.

7. Christ's Service was preceded by Prayer.

"And in the morning, rising up a great while before day, He went out, and departed into a solitary place, and there prayed" (1:35). Mark is the only one that records this. And how significant that this statement is placed in his *first* chapter, as though to let us into the secret of the uniqueness and perfectness of Christ's service!

There is much more that is peculiar to this second Gospel which we now pass over. In closing here we would call attention to the manner in which Mark concludes:—"And they (the apostles) went forth, and preached everywhere, *the Lord working with them*, and confirming the Word with signs following. Amen" (16:20). How significant and appropriate! The last view we have here of God's perfect Servant, He is still "working," now, not alone, but "with them" His servants.

Our study of this lovely view of Christ will have been in vain, unless it has brought home to our hearts with new power the admonition of God through His apostle, "Therefore, my beloved brethren, be ye stedfast, unmoveable, *always abounding in the work of the Lord,* forasmuch as ye know that your labor is not in vain in the Lord" (1 Cor. 15: 58).

THE GOSPEL OF LUKE.

THE GOSPEL OF LUKE.

THE numerical position which Luke occupies in the Sacred Canon, supplies a sure key to its interpretation. It is the third book in the New Testament, and the forty-second in the Bible as a whole. Each of these numbers are profoundly significant and suggestive in this connection. Three is the number of *manifestation,* and particularly, the manifestation of God and His activities. It is in the Three Persons of the Blessed Trinity that the one true and living God is fully revealed. Hence, also, three is the number of resurrection, for resurrection is when life is fully manifested. Appropriately, then, is Luke's Gospel the *third* book of the New Testament, for here it is we are shown, as nowhere else so fully, *God manifest in flesh*. But Luke's Gospel is also the forty-second book in the Bible as a whole, and this is, if possible, even more significant, for 42 is 7 x 6, and seven stands for perfection while six is the number of man: putting the two together we get *the Perfect Man!* And this is precisely what the Holy Spirit brings before us in this forty-second book of the Bible. What an evidence this is, not only of the Divine inspiration of Scripture but, that God has unmistakeably superintended the *placing* of the different books in the Sacred Canon just as we now have them!

Luke's Gospel is concerned with the Humanity of our Lord. In Matthew, Christ is seen *testing Israel,* and that is why his Gospel has the first place in the New Testament, as being the necessary link with the Old. In Mark, Christ appears as *serving Israel,* and that is why his Gospel is given the second place. But in Luke, the writer's scope is enlarged: here Christ is seen in racial connections as the Son *of Man,* contrasted from the sons of men. In John, Christ's highest glory is revealed, for there He is viewed as the Son of God, and, as connected not with Israel, not with men as men, but with believers. Thus we may admire the Divine wisdom in the arrangement of the four Gospels, and see the beautiful gradation in their order. Matthew is designed specially for the Jews; Mark is peculiarly suited to God's servants; Luke is adapted to men as men—all men; while John's is the one wherein the Church has found its chief delight.

Luke's Gospel, then, is the Gospel of Christ's Manhood. It shows us God manifest in flesh. It presents Christ as "The Son of Man." It views the Lord of glory as having come down to our level, entering into our conditions (sin excepted), subject to our circumstances, and living His life on the same plane as ours is lived. Yet, while He is here seen mingling with men, at every point He appears in sharp contrast from them. There was as great a difference between Christ as *the* Son of Man, and any one of us as *a son* of man, as there is now between Him as *the* Son of God, and any believer as *a son* of God. That difference was not merely relative, but absolute; not simply incidental, but essential; not one of degree, but of kind. *"The* Son of Man" predicates the *uniqueness* of His humanity. The humanity of our Lord was miraculously begotten, it was intrinsically holy in its nature, and therefore, saw not corruption in death. As *The* Son of Man, He was born as none other ever was, He lived as none other ever did, and He died as none other ever could.

The humanity of Christ, like everything else connected with His peerless person, needs to be discussed with profound reverence and care. Speculation concerning it is profane. Rash conjectures about it must not be allowed for a moment. All that we can know about it is what has been revealed in the Scriptures. Had some of our theologians adhered more rigidly to what the Holy Spirit has said on the subject, had they exercised more care in "holding fast the form of sound words," much that has been so dishonoring to our Lord had never been written. The person of the God-Man is not presented to our view for intellectual analysis, but for the worship of our hearts. It is not without good reason that we have been expressly warned, *"great* is the Mystery of Godliness. God was manifest in flesh" (1 Tim. 3:16).

As we prayerfully examine the written word it will be found that Divine care has been taken to guard the perfections of our Lord's humanity, and to bring out its holy character. This appears not only in connection with the more direct references to His person, but also in the types and prophecies of the Old Testament. The "lamb," which portrayed Him as the appointed Sacrifice for sin, must be "without spot and blemish," and the very houses wherein the lamb was eaten, must have all leaven (emblem of evil) carefully excluded from them. The "manna," which spoke of Christ as the Food for God's people, is described as being *"white"* in color (Ex. 16:31). The Meal offering, which directly pointed to the Humanity of Christ, was to be only of *"fine* flour" (Lev. 2:1), that is, flour without any grit or unevenness; moreover, it was to be presented to the Lord accompanied with "oil" and "frankincense," which were emblems of the Holy Spirit, and the fragrance of Christ's person. Joseph, the most striking of all the personal types of the Lord Jesus, was, we are told, "A *goodly person,* and well favored" (Gen. 39:6).

This same feature is noticeable in the prophecies which referred to the humanity of the Coming One. It was a "virgin" in whose womb He should be conceived (Is. 7:14). As the Incarnate One, God spake of Him thus: "Behold My Servant, whom I uphold; Mine Elect, *in whom My soul delighteth;* I have put My Spirit upon Him" (Is. 42:1). Touching the personal excellencies of the Son of Man, the Spirit of prophecy exclaimed, "Thou art *fairer than the children of men:* grace is poured into Thy lips: therefore God hath blessed Thee for ever" (Ps. 45:2). Concerning the Sinlessness of Him who was cut off out of the land of the living, it was affirmed, "He hath done *no* violence, neither was *any* deceit found in *His* mouth" (Is. 53:9). Looking forward to the time when His humanity should pass through death without corruption, it was said, *"His* leaf also *shall not wither"* (or "fade," margin), Ps. 1:3—contrast with this, *"We* all *do* fade as a leaf" (Is. 64:6).

Coming now to the New Testament, we may observe how carefully God has distinguished the Man Christ Jesus from all other men. In I Tim. 3:16 we read, "Great is the mystery of godliness: God was manifest in the flesh." It is remarkable that in the Greek there is no definite article here: what the Holy Spirit really says is, "God was manifest in flesh." Manifest in "flesh" He was, but not in *the* flesh, for *that* would point to fallen human nature, shared by all the depraved descendants of Adam. Not in *the* flesh, but in flesh, sinless and holy flesh, was God "manifest." O the marvellous minute accuracy of Scripture! In like manner we read again concerning the humanity of Christ, "What the law could not do in that it was weak through *the* flesh, God sending His own Son *in the likeness of* sin's flesh (Greek)" Rom. 8:3. The spotless and perfect humanity of the Saviour was not sinful like ours, but only after its "likeness" or outward form. As Heb. 7:26 declares He was "holy, harmless, undefiled, *separate from sinners.*" Separate from sinners He was, both in the intrinsic quality of His humanity, and in the perfect life He lived here. He "knew no sin" (2 Cor. 5:21); He "did not sin" (1 Pet. 2:22); He was "without sin" (Heb. 4:15); therefore could He say, "The prince of this world (Satan) cometh and hath *nothing* in Me" (John 14:30).

In keeping with the theme of Luke's Gospel, it is here we have the fullest particulars concerning the miraculous birth of the Lord Jesus. Here we read, "In the sixth month (how significant is this number here, for six is the number of *man*) the angel Gabriel was sent from God unto a city of Galilee, called Nazareth, To a virgin espoused to a man whose name was Joseph, of the house of David; and the virgin's name was Mary" (Luke 1:26, 27). Twice over is it here recorded that Mary was a "virgin." Continuing, we read, "And the angel came in unto her, and said, Hail, thou art highly favored, the Lord is with thee: blessed art thou among women." This troubled Mary, for she wondered at this strange salutation. The angel continued, "Fear not,

Mary: for thou hast found favor with God. And, behold, thou shalt conceive in thy womb, and bring forth a son, and shalt call His name Jesus." In reply, Mary asked, "How shall this be, seeing I know not a man?" And the angel answered, "The Holy Spirit shall come upon thee, and the power of the Highest shall overshadow thee: therefore also that holy thing which shall be born of thee shall be called the Son of God" (Luke 1:35).

The coming of the Holy Spirit "upon" a person is always, in Scripture, to effect a supernatural, a Divine work. The promise of the angel to Mary that the power of the Highest should *"overshadow"* her, suggests a double thought: she should be *protected* by God Himself, and how this promise was fulfilled Matt. 1:19, 20 informs us; while it is also a *warning* that the modus operandi of this miracle is *hidden* from us. The words of the angel to Mary "that *holy thing* which shall be born of thee," have been a sore puzzle to the commentators. Yet the meaning of this expression is very simple. It refers not, concretely, to our Lord's person, but instead, abstractly, to His humanity. It calls attention to the *uniqueness* of His humanity. It is in pointed contrast from ours. Put these words of Luke 1:35 over against another expression in Is. 64:6 and their meaning will be clear—*We* are all as an *unclean thing."* Our human nature, looked at abstractly, (that is, apart from its *personal acts*) is, essentially, "unclean," whereas that which the Son of God took unto Himself, when He became incarnate, was essentially, "holy." It was not only sinless and incapable of sinning (which is merely a *negative* affirmation), but it was inherently and positively *"holy."* Therein the humanity of Christ differed from that of Adam. Adam, in his unfallen state, was merely innocent (a *negative* quality again), but Christ was *holy*. Perhaps it may be well for us to offer a few remarks at this point concerning the Saviour's "temptation."

We are frequently hearing of preachers making the statement that our Lord *could* have yielded to the solicitations of Satan, and that to affirm He *could not* is to rob the account of His conflict with the Devil of all meaning. But this is not only a mistake, it is a serious error. It dishonors the person of our blessed Lord. It denies His impeccability. It impeaches His own declaration that Satan had "nothing" in Him—nothing to which he could appeal. *If* there had been a possibility of the Saviour yielding to the Devil that season in the wilderness, then for forty days the salvation of all God's elect (to say nothing of the outworking of God's eternal purpose) *was in jeopardy;* and surely that is unthinkable. But, it is asked, If there was no possibility of Christ yielding, wherein lay the force of the Temptation? If He could not sin, was it not a meaningless performance to allow Satan to tempt Christ at all? Such questions only betray the deplorable ignorance of those who ask them.

It ought to be well understood that the word "tempt" has a *double* significance, a primary and a secondary meaning, and it is the application of the *secondary* meaning of the term as it is used in Matthew 4 and the parallel passages, which has led so many into error on this point. The word "tempt" literally means "to stretch out" so as to *try* the strength of anything. It comes from the Latin word "tendo"—to stretch. Our English word attempt, meaning to try, brings out its significance.

"Tempt," then, *primarily* signifies "to try, test, put to the proof." It is only in its secondary meaning that it has come to signify "to solicit to evil." In Gen. 22:1 we read, "And it came to pass after these things, that *God did tempt* Abraham." But God did not solicit Abraham to evil, for, "God cannot be tempted with evil, neither tempteth He (in this sense) any man" (Jas. 1:13). So, too, we read, "Then was Jesus led up *of the Spirit* into the wilderness to be tempted of the Devil" (Matt. 4:1). The purpose of this Temptation was not to discover whether or not the Saviour would yield to Satan, but to demonstrate that He *could not*. Its design was to display His impeccability, to show forth the fact that there *was* "nothing" in Him to which Satan could appeal. It was in order that Christ might be tried and proven: just as the more you crush a rose, the more its fragrance is evidenced, so the assaults of the Devil upon the God-Man only served the more to bring out His perfections, and thus reveal Him as fully qualified to be the Saviour of sinners.

That the Saviour could not sin, *does not* rob the Temptation of its meaning, it only helps us discern its *true* meaning. It is because He was the Holy One of God that He felt the force of Satan's fiery darts as no sinful man ever could. It is impossible to find an analogy in the human realm for the Lord Jesus was absolutely unique. But let us attempt to illustrate the *principle* which is here involved. Is it true that in proportion as a man is weak morally that he feels the force of a temptation? Surely not. It is the man who is strong morally that feels the *force* of it. A man who is weakened in his moral fiber by sin, is weakened in his sensitiveness in the

WHY FOUR GOSPELS?

presence of temptation. Why does the young believer ask, "How is it that since I became a Christian I am tempted to do wrong a hundred times more than I was formerly?" The correct answer is, he is not; but the life of Christ within him has made him keener, quicker, more sensitive to the force of temptation. The illustration fails, we know; but seek to elevate the principle to an infinite height, and apply it to Christ, and then instead of saying that because He had no sin and could not sin His temptation, therefore, was meaningless, you will perhaps discover a far deeper meaning in it, and appreciate as never before the force of the words, "He Himself hath *suffered,* being tempted" (Heb. 2:18). Should it be asked further: But does not this rob the Saviour of the capacity to *sympathise* with me when *I am tempted?* The answer is, A thousand times No! But it is to be feared that this last question is really an *evasion.* Does not the questioner, deep down in his heart, *really* mean, Can Christ sympathise with me when *I yield* to temptation? The question has only to be stated thus to answer it. Being holy, Christ never sympathizes with sin or sinning. Here then is the vital difference: when Christ was tempted He "suffered," but when we are drawn away by temptation we *enjoy* it. If, however, we seek grace to sustain us while we are under temptation, and are not drawn away by it, then shall we suffer too, but *then* we also have a merciful and faithful High Priest who is able, not only to sympathise with us but to, "succor them that are tempted" (Heb. 2:18). Our digression has been rather a lengthy one, but necessary, perhaps, in a consideration of the Humanity of Christ, one postulate of which is His impeccability.

As previously stated, Luke's Gospel is *wider in its range* than either of the two which precede it, in both of which Christ is viewed in connection with Israel. But here there are no national limitations. The "Son of David" of the first Gospel, widens out into the "Son of Man" in the third Gospel. As "Son of Man" He is the *Catholic Man*. He is linked with, though separated from, the whole human race. Luke's Gospel, therefore, is in a special sense the *Gentile* Gospel, as Matthew's is the Jewish Gospel. It is not surprising to find, then, that the writer of it was himself, in all probability, a Gentile—the only one in all the Bible. It is generally conceded by scholars that Luke is an abbreviation of the Latin "Lucanus" or "Lucius." His name is twice found in the Pauline Epistles in a list of Gentile names, see 2 Tim. 4:10-12 and Philemon 24. It is also noteworthy that this third Gospel is addressed, not to a Jew, but to a Gentile, by name "Theophilus," which means "Beloved of God." It is in this Gentilish Gospel, and nowhere else, that Christ is presented as the good *"Samaritan."* Obviously, this would have been quite out of place in Matthew's Gospel, but how thoroughly accordant is it here! So, too, it is only here that we are told that "Jerusalem shall be trodden down of the *Gentiles,* until *the times of the Gentiles* be fulfilled" (Luke 21:24). And again, it is in this Gospel that, in describing End-time conditions, we learn that Christ spake to His disciples this parable: "Behold the fig tree, and all the trees" (21:29). Matthew mentions the former (24:32), as the 'fig tree' is the well known symbol of Israel, but Luke, alone, adds "and *all* the trees," thus bringing out the international scope of his Gospel. Other illustrations of this same feature will be discovered by the careful student.

Returning to the central theme of this Gospel, we may observe that "the Son of Man" links Christ with *the earth*. It is the title by which Christ most frequently referred to Himself. Not once did any one else ever address Him by this name. The first occurrence of this title is found in the Old Testament, in the 8th Psalm, where we read, "What is man that Thou art mindful of Him? and the Son of Man that Thou visitest him? For Thou hast made him a little lower than the angels, and hast crowned him with glory and honor. Thou madest him *to have dominion* over the works of Thy hands; Thou hast put all things under his feet" (vv. 4-6). The immediate reference is to Adam, in his unfallen condition, and refers to his *Headship* over all the lower orders of creation. It speaks of earthly dominion, for "Have dominion over the fish of the sea, and over the fowl of the air, and over every living thing that moveth upon the earth" (Gen. 1:28), is what God said to our first parent in the day that he was created. But from this position of "dominion" Adam fell, and it was (among other things) to recover the dominion that Adam had lost, that our Lord became incarnate. Thus the eighth Psalm, as is evident from its quotation in Hebrews 2, finds its ultimate fulfillment in "the Second Man." But, before this Second Man could be "crowned with glory and honor," He must first humble Himself and pass through the portals of death. Thus the "Son of Man" title speaks first of humiliation, and ultimately of dominion and glory.

"The Son of Man" occurs 88 times in the New Testament (which is a very significant number, for

8 signifies *a new beginning,* and it is by the Second Man the beginning of the new "Dominion" will be established), and it is deeply interesting and instructive to trace out the connections in which it occurs. It is found for the first time in the New Testament in Matt. 8:20, where the Saviour says, "The foxes have holes, and the birds of the air have nests; *but the Son of Man hath not where to lay His head."* Here attention is called to the depths of humiliation into which the Beloved of the Father had entered: the One who shall yet have complete dominion over all the earth, when here before, was but a homeless Stranger. The second occurrence of this title helps to define its scope—"The Son of Man hath power *on earth* to forgive sins" (Matt. 9:6). The last time it is found in Matthew's Gospel is in 26:64 —"Hereafter shall ye see the Son of Man sitting on the right hand of power, and coming in the clouds of heaven." Here we are carried forward to the time when the Lord Jesus shall return to these scenes, not in weakness and humiliation, but in power and glory. In John 3:13 there is a statement made which proves that the San of Man was God as well, "And no man hath ascended up to Heaven, but He that came down from Heaven, even *the Son of Man which is in Heaven."* Nowhere in the Epistles (save in Heb. 2 where Ps. 8 is quoted) is this title found, for the Church has a *heavenly* calling and destiny, and is linked to the Son of God in Heaven, and not to the Son of Man as He is related to the earth. The last time this title occurs in Scripture is in Rev. 14:14, where we read, "And I looked, and behold a white cloud, and upon the cloud One sat like unto the Son of Man, having on His head *a golden crown."* What a contrast is this

from the first mention of this title in the New Testament where we read of Him not having where to lay "His head"!

It is now high time for us to turn from these generalizings and consider some features of Luke's Gospel in more detail. To begin with, we may observe, as others have noticed, how distinctive and characteristic is the Preface to this third Gospel: "Forasmuch as many have taken in hand to set forth in order a declaration of those things which are most surely believed among us, even as they delivered them unto us, which from the beginning were eyewitnesses, and ministers of the Word: It seemed good to me also, having had perfect understanding of all things from the very first to write unto thee, in order, most excellent Theophilus, that thou mightest know the certainty of those things, wherein thou hast been instructed" (1:1-4).

What a contrast is this from what we have at the commencement of the other Gospels. Here more pronouncedly than elsewhere, we see the human element in the communication of God's revelation to us. The human instrument is brought plainly before us. Luke speaks of his personal knowledge of that of which he is about to treat. He refers to what others had done before him in this direction, but feels the need of a more orderly and full setting forth of those things which were most surely believed. But apparently he was quite unconscious of the fact, as he sat down to write to his friend Theophilus, that he was being "moved" (better, "borne along") by the Holy Spirit, or that he was about to communicate that which should be of lasting value to the whole Church of God. Instead, the Divine Inspirer is hidden here, and only the human penman is seen. Strikingly appropriate is this in the Gospel which treats not of the official glories of Christ, nor of His Deity, but of His *Manhood*. There is a marvellous analogy between the written Word of God and the Incarnate Word, the details of which are capable of being extended indefinitely. Just as Christ was the God-Man, Divine yet human, so the Holy Scriptures though given "by inspiration of God" were, nevertheless, communicated through human channels; but, just as Christ in becoming Man did so without being contaminated by sin, so God's revelation has come to us through human medium without being defiled by any of their imperfections. Moreover, just as it is here in Luke's Gospel that our Lord's humanity is brought so prominently before us, so it is here that the human element in the giving of the Holy Scriptures is most plainly to be seen.

There are many other things of interest and importance to be found in this first chapter of Luke which we cannot now consider in detail, but we would point out, in passing, how the *human* element prevails throughout. We may notice, for instance, how that here God is seen on more intimate terms with those whom He addresses than in Matt. 1. There, when communicating with Joseph, He did so in "dreams," but here, when sending a message to Zacharias, it is by an angel, who speaks to the father of the Baptist face to face. Still more intimate is God's communication to Mary, for here the angel speaks not to the mother of our Lord in the temple, but more familiarly, in the home—an intimation of how near God was about to come to men in His marvellous grace. Again; far more is told us of Mary here than elsewhere, and Luke is the only one who records her song of joy which followed the great Annunciation, as he alone records the prophecy of Zacharias, uttered on the occasion of the naming of his illustrious son. Thus, the emotions of the human heart are here manifested as they were expressed in song and praise.

The opening verses of Luke 2 are equally characteristic and distinctive. Here we are told, "And it came to pass in those days, that there went out a decree from Caesar Augustus, that all the world should be taxed. And this taxing was first made when Cyrenius was governor of Syria. And all went to be taxed, every one into his own city. And Joseph also went up from Galilee, out of the city of Nazareth, into Judea, unto the city of David, which is called Bethlehem; because he was of the house and lineage of David: to be taxed with Mary his espoused wife" (Luke 2:1-5). We shall look in vain for anything like this in the other Gospels. Here the Lord of glory is contemplated not as the One who had come to reign, but instead, as One who had descended to the level of other men, as One whose mother and legal father were subject to the common taxation. This would have been altogether out of keeping with the theme and scope of Matthew's Gospel, and a point of no interest in Mark, but how thoroughly in accord with the character of Luke's Gospel!

"And she brought forth her firstborn son, and wrapped Him in swaddling clothes, and laid Him in a manger; because there was no room for them in the inn" (Luke 2:7). Luke is the only one of the four evangelists who tells us of this—a point of touching interest concerning His humanity, and one that is worthy of our reverent contemplation. *Why* was it the Father suffered His blessed Son, now incarnate, to be born in a stable? *Why* were the cattle of the field His first companions? What spiritual lessons are we intended to learn from His being placed in a manger? Weighty questions are these admitting, perhaps, of at least a sevenfold answer.

(a) He was laid in a manger because there was *no room in the inn*. How solemnly this brings out *the world's estimate* of the Christ of God. There was no appreciation of His amazing condescension. He was not wanted. It is so still. There is no room for Him in the schools, in society, in the business world, among the great throngs of pleasure seekers, in the political realm, in the newspapers, nor in many of the churches. It is only history repeating itself. All that the world gave the Saviour, was a stable for His cradle, a cross on which to die, and a borrowed grave to receive His murdered body.

(b) He was laid in a manger to demonstrate *the extent of His Poverty*. "For ye know the grace of our Lord Jesus Christ, that, though He was rich, yet for your sakes He became poor, that ye through His poverty might be rich" (2 Cor. 8:9). *How* "poor" He became, was thus manifested at the beginning. The One who, afterwards, had not where to lay His head, who had to *ask for* a penny when He would reply to His critics about the question of tribute, and who had to use another man's house when instituting the Holy Supper, was, from the first, a homeless Stranger here. And the "manger" was the earliest evidence of this.

(c) He was laid in a manger in order to be *Accessible to all*. Had He been born in a palace, or in some room in the Temple, few could have reached

Him without the formality of first gaining permission from those who would have been in attendance at such places. But none would have any difficulty in obtaining access to a *stable;* there He would be within easy reach of poor and rich alike. Thus, from the beginning, He was easy of approach. No intermediaries had first to be passed in order to reach Him. No priest had to be interviewed before *entre* could be obtained to His presence. Thus it was then; and so it is now, thank God.

(d) He was laid in a manger so as to foreshadow *the Character of those among whom He had come.* The stable was the place for beasts of the field, and it was into *their* midst the newly-born Saviour came. And how well did they symbolize the moral character of men! The beasts of the field are devoid of any spiritual life, and so have no knowledge of God. Such, too, was the condition of both Jews and Gentiles. And how *beastlike* in character *were* those into whose midst the Saviour came: stupid and stubborn as the ass or mule, cunning and cruel as the fox, grovelling and filthy as the swine, and ever thirsting for His blood as the more savage of the animals. Fittingly, then, was He placed amid the beasts of the field at His birth.

(e) He was laid in a manger to show *His contempt for Worldly riches and pomp.* We had thought it more fitting for the Christ of God to be born in a palace, and laid in a cradle of gold, lined with costly silks. Ah, but as He Himself reminds us in this same Gospel, "that which is highly esteemed among men, is abomination in the sight of God" (Luke 16:15). And what an exemplification of this truth was given when the infant Saviour was placed, not in a cradle of gold but, in an humble manger.

(f) He was laid in a manger to mark *His identification with human suffering and wretchedness.* The One born was "The Son *of Man."* He had left the heights of Heaven's glory and had descended to our level, and here we behold Him entering the human lot at its lowest point. Adam was first placed in a garden, surrounded by the exquisite beauties of Nature as it left the hands of the Creator. But sin had come in, and with sin all its sad consequences of suffering and wretchedness. Therefore, does the One who had come here to recover and restore what the first man lost, appear first, in surroundings which spoke of abject need and wretchedness; just as a little later we find Him taken down into Egypt, in order that God might call His Son from the same place as where His people Israel commenced their national history in misery and wretchedness. Thus did the Man of Sorrows identify Himself with human suffering.

(g) He was laid in a manger because such was *the place of Sacrifice.* The manger was the place where vegetable life was sacrificed to sustain animal life. Fitting place was this, then, for Him who had come to be the great Sacrifice, laying down His life for His people, that we might through His death be made alive. Remarkably suggestive, therefore, and full of emblematic design, was the place appointed by God to receive the infant body of the incarnate Saviour.

It is only in Luke's Gospel that we read of the shepherds who kept watch over their flocks by night, and to whom the angel of the Lord appeared, saying, "Fear not: for, behold, I bring you good tidings of great joy, which shall be to all people. For unto you is born this day in the city of David a

Saviour, which is Christ the Lord" (2:10, 11). Note that the One born is here spoken of not as "The King of the Jews," but as *"a Saviour, which is Christ the Lord"*—titles which reach out beyond the confines of Israel, and take in the Gentiles too.

Again, it is only here in Luke that we behold the Saviour as a Boy of twelve going up to Jerusalem, and being found in the Temple "sitting in the midst of the doctors, both hearing them, *and asking them questions*" (2:46). How intensely human is this! Yet side by side with it there is a strong hint given that He was more than human, for we read, "And all that heard Him were astonished at His understanding and answers." So, too, it is only here that we are told, "And He went down with them (His parents), and was *subject unto them*" (2:51). How this brings out the excellencies of His humanity, perfectly discharging the responsibilities of every relationship which He sustained to men as well as to God! And how strikingly appropriate is the closing verse of this chapter—"And Jesus *increased* in wisdom and stature and in favor with God and man"! There is nothing like this in any of the other Gospels; but Luke's would have been incomplete without it. What proofs are these that Luke, as the others, was guided by the Spirit of God in the selection of his materials!

Luke 3 opens by presenting to us the person and mission of John the Baptist. Matthew and Mark have both referred to this, but Luke adds to the picture his own characteristic lines. Only here do we read that it was "in the fifteenth year of the reign of Tiberius Cæsar, Pontius Pilate being governor of Judea, and Herod being tetrarch of Galilee, and his brother Philip tetrarch of Iturea and of the region of Trachonitis, and Lysanias the tetrarch of Abilene, Annas and Caiaphas being the high priests, the Word of God came unto John, the son of Zacharias in the wilderness" (3:1, 2)—points of historic interest in connection with these *human* relationships. So, too, it is only here that we read of other human relationships of "the people" who asked John "What shall we do?" (3:10), of the "publicans" who asked him the same question (3:12), and of "the soldiers" who came to him with a similar query (3:14). It is also to be noted, that only here is the Lord Jesus directly linked with "all the people" when *He* was baptized, for we read, "Now when *all the people* were baptized, it came to pass that Jesus *also* being baptized" (3:21), thus showing Him as the One who had come down to the common level. And again, it is only here we are told of the *age* of the Saviour when He entered upon His public ministry (3:23), this being another point of interest in connection with His *humanity*.

Luke 3 closes with a record of the Genealogy of the Son of Man, and noticeable are the differences between what we have here, and what is found in Matt. 1. There, it is the royal genealogy of the Son of David, here it is His strictly personal genealogy. There, it is His line of descent through Joseph which is given, here it is His ancestry through Mary. There, His genealogy is traced forwards from Abraham, here it is followed backwards to Adam. This is very striking, and brings out in an unmistakable manner the respective character and scope of each Gospel. Matthew is showing Christ's relation to Israel, and therefore he goes back no farther than to Abraham, the father of the Jewish people; but here, it is His connection with the human race that is before us, and hence his genealogy in Luke is traced right back to Adam, the father of the human family. But notice, particularly, that at the close it is said, "Adam was the son *of God*" (3:38). Thus the humanity of Christ is here traced not merely back to Adam, but through Adam directly to God Himself. How marvellously this agrees with the words of the Lord Jesus as found in Heb. 10:5—"A body *hast Thou* prepared Me"!

Luke 4 opens by telling us "And Jesus being full of the Holy Spirit returned from Jordan, and was led by the Spirit into the wilderness, being tempted forty days of the Devil." Only here do we learn that the Saviour was "full of the Holy Spirit" as He returned from the Jordan. Then follows the account of the Temptation. It will be observed by the close student that between Matthew and Luke there is a difference in *the order* of mention of Satan's three attacks upon Christ. In Matthew the order is, first the asking of the Lord Jesus to turn the stones into bread, second the bidding Him cast Himself down from the pinnacle of the Temple, and third the offer to Him of all the kingdoms of this world on the condition of worshipping Satan. But here in Luke we have first the request to make the stones into bread, second the offer of the kingdoms of the world, and third the challenge for Him to cast Himself down from the pinnacle of the temple. The reason for this variation is not hard to find. In Matthew, the order is arranged *climactically,* so as to make Rulership over all the kingdoms of the world the final bait which the Devil dangled before the Son of David. But in Luke we have, no doubt, the *chronological* order, the order in which they actually occurred, and these correspond with the order of temptation of the first man and his wife in Eden, where the appeal was made, as here in Luke, to the lust of the flesh, the lust of the eyes, and the pride of life—see 1 John 2:16 and compare Gen. 3:6. We may also note that Luke is the only one to tell us that "Jesus returned in the power of the Spirit into Galilee" (4:14), showing that the old Serpent had utterly failed to disturb the perfect fellowship which existed between the incarnate Son of God upon earth and His Father in Heaven. After the horrible conflict was over, the Lord Jesus returned to Galilee in the *unabated* "power of the Spirit."

Following the account of the Temptation, Luke next tells us, "And He came to Nazareth, where He had been brought up: and, as His custom was, He went into the synagogue on the Sabbath day, and stood up for to read" (4:16). Luke, again, is the only one that mentions this, it being another point of interest in connection with our Lord's Manhood, informing us, as it does, of the place where He had been "brought up," and showing us how He had there been wont to occupy Himself on each Sabbath day. In the words that follow there is a small line in the picture which is very significant and suggestive: "And there was delivered unto Him the book of the prophet Isaiah. And when He had opened the book, *He found the place* where it was written, The Spirit of the Lord is upon Me" etc. The book, be it noted, did not open magically at the page He desired to read from, but, like any other, the Son of Man *turned the pages* until He had "found the place" required!

Others have called attention to another thing which occurred on this occasion and which was profoundly suggestive. There in the synagogue at Nazareth the Saviour read from the opening words of Isaiah 61, and it will be found by comparing the record of the prophet with the Lord's reading as recorded in Luke 4, that He stopped at a most significant point. Isaiah says the Spirit of the Lord was upon Him to "preach good tidings unto the meek * * to proclaim the acceptable year of the Lord, and the day of vengeance of our God;" but in Luke 4 we find the Saviour read that the Spirit of the Lord was upon Him to "preach the gospel to the poor * * to proclaim the acceptable year of the Lord," *and there He stopped,* for immediately following we are told, "He closed the book." He ceased His reading from Isaiah in the midst of a sentence; He concluded at a comma! Why was it that He did not complete the verse, and add, "The Day of Vengeance of our God"? The answer is, Because such did not fall within the scope of His mission at His first Advent. The "Day of Vengeance" is yet future. The Lord Jesus was setting us an example of "rightly dividing the Word of Truth" (2 Tim. 2:15). As the Saviour closed the book that day in Nazareth's synagogue, He declared, "This day is this Scripture fulfilled in your ears" (Luke 4:21), and *that* which was then "fulfilled" was the portion He had read to them from Isaiah 61:1, 2; the remainder of Is. 61:2 was not then fulfilled, for it has to do with that which is yet future: hence, He read it not. It should be added that the next time we find the Lord Jesus with a "book" in His hands is in Rev. 5:7, and there we read of Him *opening* it—see Rev. 6:1 etc.—and the striking thing is that when the Lord opens that book the Day of God's Vengeance, so long delayed, then commences! These points have been brought out by others before us, but we have not seen it intimated that *Luke* is the only one of the four Evangelists to refer to this incident. Not only was there a *dispensational* reason why the Lord Jesus read not the whole of Is. 61:2 in the Nazareth synagogue that day, but it was peculiarly fitting that the one whose happy task it was to present the human perfections of Christ, should note our Lord's silence concerning the Day of *God's* "vengeance"!

It is beyond our present purpose to attempt even a running exposition of each chapter of this third Evangel. We are not seeking to be exhaustive, but simply suggestive, calling attention to some of the more outstanding features of Luke's Gospel. There is so much here that is not found in the other three Gospels, that to examine in detail every distinctive feature would call for a large volume. As this would defeat our object, we shall be content to single out a few things here and there.

Luke 7 records the raising of the widow of Nain's son. None of the others mention this. There are several lines in this picture which serve to bring out that which is central in Luke's Gospel, namely, human need, human relationships, and human sympathies. Thus we may note that the one here raised by Christ was "the only son of his mother" and that she was a "widow;" that when the Lord saw her "He had compassion on her" and that He bade her "weep not"; that before He commanded the dead to "Arise," He first "came and touched the bier," and that after the dead one was restored to life, the Saviour "delivered him to his mother."

In Luke 8:2, 3 we are told, "And certain women which had been healed of evil spirits and infirmities, Mary called Magdalene, out of whom went seven demons, and Joanna the wife of Chuza, Herod's steward, and Susanna, and many others, which *ministered unto Him of their substance."* How this shows us the place which our blessed Lord had taken as the Son of Man! Nothing like this is found in the other Gospels, and that for a very good reason. It would have been beneath the dignity of the *King* of the Jews to be "ministered unto" with the substance of women; it would be out of place in Mark's Gospel, for there the Holy Spirit shows us that the *Servant* must look to God only for the supply of His every need; while John, of course, would not mention it, for he sets forth the *Divine* glories of our Lord. But it is perfectly appropriate, and illuminative too, in the Gospel which treats of Christ's *humanity*.

Above we have noted that Luke informs us the one raised from death by Christ at Nain was a widow's "only son," and we may now notice two other examples from this Gospel where the same feature is mentioned. The first is in connection with the daughter of Jairus. Matthew says, "While He spake these things unto them, behold, there came a certain ruler, and worshipped Him saying, *My daughter* is even now dead" (9:18). Mark tells us, "Behold, there cometh one of the rulers of the synagogue, Jairus by name; and when he saw Him, he fell at His feet, And besought Him, saying, *My little daughter* lieth at the point of death" (5:22, 23). But Luke gives additional information, "And, behold, there came a man named Jairus, and he was a ruler of the synagogue: and he fell down at Jesus' feet, and besought Him that He would come into his house: for he had *one only daughter*, about twelve years of age, and she lay a dying" (8:41, 42). The second example is in connection with the demon-possessed child, whose father sought relief at the hands of Christ's disciples. Matthew says, "And when they were come to the multitude, there came to Him a certain man, kneeling down to Him, and saying, Lord, have mercy on *my son:* for he is lunatick, and sore vexed: for ofttimes he falleth into the fire, and oft into the water. And I brought him to Thy disciples, and they could not cure him" (17: 14-16). But Luke tells us, "And, behold, a man of the company cried out, saying, Master, I beseech Thee, look upon my son: *for he is mine only child.* And, lo, a spirit taketh him, and he suddenly crieth out; and it teareth him that he foameth again, and bruising him hardly departeth from him. And I besought Thy disciples to cast him out; and they could not" (9:38-40). Thus in each case Luke calls attention to the fact that it was an "only child" that was healed, thereby appealing to *human sympathies.*

Luke is the only one who records the exquisite story of the Good Samaritan ministering to the wounded traveller, and there are many lines in the picture of this incident which bring out, strikingly, the distinctive character of this third Gospel. First, we are shown the traveller himself falling among thieves, who strip him of his raiment, wound him, and depart, leaving him half dead. How this brings out the lawlessness, the avarice, the brutality, and the heartlessness of fallen human nature! Next, we hear of the priest who *saw* the pitiable state of the wounded traveller, lying helpless by the road, yet did he "pass by on the other side." The priest was followed by a Levite who, though he "came and *looked on*" on the poor man that was in such sore need of help, also "passed by on the other side." Thus we behold the selfishness, the callousness, the

WHY FOUR GOSPELS?

cruel indifference of even religious men toward one who had such a claim upon their sympathies. In blessed contrast from these, we are shown the grace of the Saviour who, under the figure of a "Samaritan," is here seen moved "with compassion" as He came to where the poor traveller lay. Instead of passing by on the other side, *He* goes to him, binds up his wounds, sets him on His own beast, and brings him to an inn, where full provision is made for him. So does this incident, summarize as it were, the scope of this entire Gospel, by showing the infinite contrast that existed between the perfect Son of Man and the fallen and depraved sons of men.

In Luke 11 we read of the unclean spirit who goes out of a man, and later, returns to his house, to find it "swept and garnished." Then, we are told, this unclean spirit takes with him seven other spirits more wicked than himself, and they "enter in and dwell there; and the last state of that man is worse than the first" (11:24-26). Matthew also refers to this in 12:43-45 in almost identical language, but it is very significant to observe that Luke omits a sentence with which Matthew closes his narrative. There in Matt. 12 we find the Lord applied the incident to the Jewish nation by saying, "Even so shall it be also unto *this wicked generation*" (or "race"). This was the *dispensational* application, which *limits* it to Israel. But appropriately does Luke *omit* these qualifying words, for in his Gospel this incident has a wider application, a *moral* application, representing the condition of a more extensive class, namely, those who hear the Gospel, and *reform,* but who are never regenerated. Such may clean up their houses, but though they are "swept and garnished," yet are they still *empty*—the Spirit of God does not indwell them! They are like the foolish virgins, who, though they mingled with the wise virgins and carried the lamp of public profession, yet had they *no oil* (emblem of the Holy Spirit) in their vessels. Such cases of reformation though at first they appear to be genuine instances of regeneration, ultimately prove to be but counterfeits, and at the last their condition is worse than it was at the beginning—they have been deceived by their own treacherous hearts and deluded and blinded by Satan, and in consequence, are far harder to reach with the Truth of God.

In Luke 12 we have an incident recorded which is similar in principle to Luke's notice of our Lord's omission of the closing words of Is. 61:2 when reading from this scripture in the synagogue at Nazareth. Here we find that a certain man came to Christ and said, "Master, speak to my brother, that he divide the inheritance with me" (12:13). But the Master refused to grant this request and said, "Man, who made Me a judge or a divider over you?" The reason why Luke is the only one to mention this is easily seen. It would have been incongruous for Matthew to have referred to an incident wherein the Lord Jesus *declined* to occupy the place of authority and act as the administrator, of an inheritance; as it would have been equally out of place for Mark to have noticed this case where one should have asked the Servant to officiate as "judge and divider." But it is fitting it should have found a place in this Third Gospel, for the words of Christ on this occasion, "Who made *Me* a judge or a divider *over* you?" only show us, once more, the lowly place which He had taken as "The Son of Man."

WHY FOUR GOSPELS? 117

In Luke 14 there is recorded a parable which is found nowhere else: "And He put forth a parable to those which were bidden, when He marked how they chose out the chief rooms; saying unto them, When thou art bidden of any man to a wedding, sit not down in the highest room, lest a more honorable man than thou be bidden of him; And he that bade thee and him come and say to thee, Give this man place; and thou begin with shame to take the lowest room. But when thou art bidden, go and sit down in the lowest room; that when he that bade thee cometh, he may say unto thee, Friend, go up higher: then shalt thou have worship (or "glory") in the presence of them that sit at meat with thee. For whosoever exalteth himself shall be abased; and he that humbleth himself shall be exalted" (vv. 7-11). How thoroughly is this parable in accord with the character and scope of Luke's Gospel! First, it ministers a much needed rebuke upon the general tendency of fallen human nature to seek out the best places and aim at positions of honor and glory. Secondly, it inculcates the spirit of meekness and modesty, admonishing us to take the lowly place. And thirdly, it is an obvious shadowing forth of that which the Lord of glory had done Himself, leaving as He had, the position of dignity and glory in Heaven, and taking the "lowest" place of all down here.

In accordance with the fact that Luke's Gospel is the *third* book of the New Testament (the number which stands for *manifestation*), we may notice that in the fifteenth chapter we have a parable which reveals to us the Three Persons of the Godhead, each actively engaged in the salvation of a sinner. It is very striking that it is *one* parable in *three* parts which, taken together, makes fully manifest the One true God in the Person of the Father, the Son, and the Holy Spirit.

Luke 15 may well be entitled, God seeking and saving the lost. In the third part of this parable, which deals with the "prodigal Son," we are shown the sinner actually coming into the presence of the Father, and there receiving a cordial welcome, being suitably clothed, and given a place at His table in happy fellowship. In what *precedes* we learn of that which was necessary on the part of God *before* the sinner could thus be reconciled. The second part of the parable brings before us *the work of the Holy Spirit,* going after the one dead in sins and illuminating him, and this under the figure of a woman who, with a *light* in her hand (emblematic of the Lamp of God's Word), seeks diligently till she finds that which was lost. Notice, particularly, that her work was *inside* the house, just as the Holy Spirit works *within* the sinner. In the first part of the parable we are shown that which preceded the present work of God's Spirit. The ministry of the Spirit is the complement to *the Work of Christ,* hence, at the beginning of the chapter, the Saviour Himself is before us, under the figure of the Shepherd, who went forth to seek and to save the sheep that was lost. Thus, the first part of the parable tells of God's work *for* us, as the second tells of God's work *in* us, the third part making known the blessed result and happy sequel. So, in this one parable in three parts, we have revealed the One God in the Three Persons of the Holy Trinity, *fully manifested* in the work of seeking and saving the lost.

In full accord with what has just been before us

in Luke 15, though in marked and solemn contrast, we find that in the next chapter the Lord Jesus *makes fully manifest* the state of the lost after death. Nowhere else in the four Gospels do we find, as here, the lifting of the veil which separates and hides from us the condition of those who have passed into the next world. Here the Lord gives us a specimen case of the present torments of the lost, in the experiences of the "rich man" after death. We read "In Hell he lift up his eyes, being in torments, and seeth Abraham afar off, and Lazarus in his bosom. And he cried and said, Father Abraham, have mercy on me, and send Lazarus that he may dip the tip of his finger in water, and cool my tongue; for I am tormented in this flame. But Abraham said, Son, remember that thou in thy lifetime receivest thy good things, and Lazarus evil things: but now he is comforted, and thou art tormented. And beside all this, between us and you there is a great gulf fixed: so that they which would pass from hence to you cannot; neither can they pass to us, that would come from thence" (vv. 23-26). Here we learn that the damned, even now, are in a place of suffering; that they are "in torments;" that the misery of their awful lot is accentuated by being enabled to "see" the happy portion of the redeemed; that there is, however, an impassible gulf fixed between the saved and the lost, which makes it impossible for the one to go to the other; that memory is still active in those that are in Hell, so that they are reminded of the opportunities wasted, while they were upon earth; that they cry for mercy and beg for water to allay their fiery sufferings, but that this is denied them. Unspeakably solemn is this, and a most pointed warning to all still upon earth to "flee from the wrath to come" and to take refuge in the only One who can deliver from it.

Passing on now to the nineteenth chapter we may observe how Luke there records something that is absent from the other Gospels. "And when He was come near, He beheld the city, *and wept over it,* Saying, If thou hadst known, even thou, at least in this thy day, the things which belong unto thy peace! but now they are hid from thine eyes" (vv. 41, 42). How this brings out the human sympathies of the Saviour! As He looked upon Jerusalem, and foresaw the miseries which were shortly to be its portion, the Son of Man wept. He was no stoic, but One whose heart was full of compassion for the sufferers of earth.

In drawing to a close, we would notice seven features which are particularly prominent in this Gospel, and which are in striking accord with its particular theme and scope:—

1. The full description here given of fallen human nature.

Luke's is the Gospel of our Lord's Manhood, and, as He is the true Light shining amid the darkness, it is here also that the characteristics of *our* corrupt human nature are shown up as nowhere else. Luke's special design is to present the Lord Jesus as the Son of Man *contrasted from the sons of men.* Hence it is that the depravity, the impotency, the degradation and the spiritual deadness of all the members of Adam's fallen race is brought out here with such fullness and clearness. It is here, and here only, we read that, until the miracle-working power of God intervened, the mother of John the Baptist was *barren*—apt symbol of fallen human nature with its total absence of spiritual fruit; and that his father, though a priest, was filled with *unbelief* when God's messenger announced to him the forth-coming miracle. It is only here that we read of all the world being "taxed" (Luke 2:1), which tells, in suggestive symbol, of the *burdens* imposed by Satan on his captive subjects. It is only here that we read that when Mary brought forth her Son, there was "no room for them in the inn," signifying the world's rejection of the Saviour from the beginning. It is only here we are told that when the Lord Jesus came to Nazareth and read in the synagogue from the prophet Isaiah, adding a comment of His own, that "All they in the synagogue, when they heard these things, were filled with wrath, And rose up, and thrust Him out of the city, and led Him unto the brow of the hill whereon their city was built, that they might cast Him down headlong" (4:28, 29): thus did those who ought to have known Him the best, manifest the terrible enmity of the carnal mind against God and His Christ. It is only here that we read, "And it came to pass, when He was in a certain city, behold a man *full* of leprosy: who seeing Jesus fell on his face, and besought Him, saying, Lord, if Thou wilt, Thou canst make me clean" (5:12). In the other Gospels reference is made to this same incident, but Luke alone tells us that the subject of this miracle was *full* of leprosy. "Leprosy" is the well known figure of *sin,* and it is only in Luke that man's *total* depravity is fully revealed. It is only in Luke that we hear of the disciples of Christ asking permission to call down fire from Heaven to consume those who received not the Saviour (9:51-55). It is only here that Christ, in the well known parable of the Good Samaritan, portrays the abject condition of the natural man, under the figure of the one who, having fallen among thieves, had been stript of his raiment, sorely wounded, and left by the wayside half dead. It is only here that we read of the Rich Fool who declared, "I will say to my soul, Soul, thou hast much goods laid up for many years; take thine ease, eat, drink, and be merry" (12:19), for such is the invariable tendency of the boastful human heart. So, too, it is only here that in Luke 15 the sinner is likened unto a lost sheep— an animal so senseless that once it is lost, it only continues to stray farther and farther away from the fold. It is only here that we find the Saviour drawing that matchless picture of the Prodigal Son, who so accurately depicts the sinner away from God, having wasted his substance in riotous living, and who, reduced to want, finds nothing in the far country to feed upon, except the husks which the swine did eat. It is only here that we learn of the heartless indifference of the rich man who neglected the poor wretch that lay at his gate full of sores. It is only here that the self-righteousness of man is fully disclosed in the person of the Pharisee in the Temple (Luke 18). And so we might go on. But sufficient has been said to prove our statement at the head of this paragraph.

2. The Manner in which Luke introduces his Parables etc.

In perfect accord with the character and scope of his Gospel, we find that Luke introduces most of his parables, also various incidents narrated by him, as well as certain portions of our Lord's teachings, in a way quite peculiar to himself. By comparing the parallel passages in the other Gospels, and by noting the words we now place in italics, this will be apparent to the reader.

In Luke 5:12, we are told, that *"a man* full of leprosy" came to Christ to be healed, whereas Matthew, when describing the same incident, merely says, "there came *a leper"* to Him (8:2). Again, in 8:27 we read, "When He went forth to land, there met Him out of the city, *a certain man,* which had demons a long time, and ware no clothes, neither abode in any house, but in the tombs;" whereas Matt. 8:28 reads, "And when He was come to the other side into the country of the Gergesenes, there met Him (not "two men," but) *two possessed with demons* coming out of the tombs" etc. Again, in 8:41 we read, "There came *a man* named Jairus, and he was a ruler of the synagogue: and he fell down at Jesus' feet," whereas Mark 5:22 says, "There cometh one of the rulers of the synagogue, Jairus by name; and when he saw Him, he fell at His feet." In Luke 9:57 we read, "And it came to pass, that, as they went in the way, *a certain man* said unto Him, Lord, I will follow Thee whithersoever Thou goest," whereas Matt. 8:19 reads, "And a certain *scribe* came, and said unto Him, Master, I will follow Thee whithersoever Thou goest." In Luke 9:62 we find that the Lord said, "No *man* (not "disciple," be it noted), having put his hand to the plough, and looking back, is fit for the kingdom of God." In 19:35 we read, "As He was come nigh unto Jericho, a certain *blind man* sat by the wayside begging," but in Mark 10:46 we are told, "As He went out of Jericho with His disciples and a great number of people, *blind Bartimaeus,* the son of Timaeus, sat by the wayside begging."

Coming now to the parables, note the striking way

in which they are introduced here: "And He spake also a parable unto them: No *man* putteth a piece of a new garment upon an old" etc. (5:36). "A certain *man* went down from Jerusalem to Jericho, and fell among thieves" etc. (10:30). "And He spake a parable unto them, saying, The ground of a certain rich *man* brought forth plentifully" etc. (12:16). "He spake also this parable: A certain *man* had a fig tree planted in his vineyard" etc. (13:6). "Then said He unto him, A certain *man* made a great supper" etc. (14:16). "And He spake this parable unto them, saying, What *man* of you, having a hundred sheep" etc. (15:3, 4). "And He said, A certain *man* had two sons" etc. (15:11). "And He said also unto His disciples, There was a certain rich *man*, which had a steward" etc. (16:1). "There was a certain rich *man*, which was clothed in purple and fine linen" etc. (16:19). "And He spake a parable to them to this end, that *men* (not "believers") ought always to pray, and not to faint" etc. (18:1). "Then began He to speak to the people this parable; A certain *man* planted a vineyard" etc. (20:9). "And He spake also this parable unto certain which trusted in themselves that they were righteous, and despised others. Two *men* went up into the Temple to pray" etc. (18:9, 10). Thus we see how the *human* element is emphasized here.

3. The references to Christ as "The Son of Man."

It is only in this Gospel we read that the Saviour said to the Pharisees, "The days will come, when ye shall desire to see one of the days of *the Son of Man*, and ye shall not see it" (17:22). It is only in this Gospel we find that the Saviour put the question, "When *the Son of Man* cometh, shall He find faith on the earth?" (18:8). It is only in this Gospel we find that the Saviour said to His followers, "Watch ye therefore, and pray always, that ye may be accounted worthy to escape all these things that shall come to pass, and to stand before *the Son of Man*" (21:36). And it is only in this Gospel we find that the Saviour said to Judas in the garden, "Betrayest thou *the Son of Man* with a kiss?" (22:14).

It is, perhaps even more striking to notice that Luke records a number of instances where our Lord referred to Himself as "The Son of Man" where, in the parallel passages in the other Gospels this title is omitted. For example, in Matt. 16:21 we read, "From that time forth began Jesus to show unto His disciples, how that He must go unto Jerusalem, and suffer many things of the elders and chief priests and scribes, and be killed, and be raised again the third day;" whereas, in Luke 9:22 we learn that He said unto His disciples, *"The Son of Man* must suffer many things, and be rejected of the elders and chief priests and scribes, and be slain, and be raised the third day." Again; in Matt. 5:11 the Lord said to His disciples, "Blessed are ye, when men shall revile you, and persecute you, and shall say all manner of evil against you falsely, *for My sake;*" whereas, in the parallel passage in Luke we read, "Blessed are ye, when men shall hate you, and when they shall separate you from their company, and shall reproach you, and cast out your name as evil, *for the Son of Man's sake"* (6:22). Again; in Matt. 10:32 we read, "But whosoever shall confess Me before men, him will *I confess* before My Father which is in Heaven;" whereas in Luke 12:8 we are told, "Whosoever shall confess Me before men, him shall *the Son of Man confess* before the angels of God." Once more; in John 3:17 we are told, "For

God sent not *His Son* into the world to condemn the world; but that the world through Him might be saved;" whereas, in Luke 9:56 we read, "For *the Son of Man* is not come to destroy men's lives, but to save them." How these examples bring out the *verbal* perfections of Holy Writ!

4. The Lord is referred to as "the Friend" of publicans and sinners.

It is only Luke who tells us, "And Levi made Him a great feast in his own house: and there was a great company of *publicans* and of others that sat down with them" (5:29). It is only here we learn that Christ said to the querulous Jews, "For John the Baptist came neither eating bread nor drinking wine, and ye say, He hath a demon. The Son of Man is come eating and drinking; and ye say, Behold a gluttonous man, and a winebibber, *a Friend of publicans and sinners!*" (7:33, 34). It is only in this Gospel we find that the Saviour's critics openly murmured, and said, "This Man *receiveth sinners,* and eateth with them" (15:2). And it is only here we are told that because Zaccheus had joyfully received the Saviour into his house "they all murmured, saying, That He was gone to be guest with *a man that is a sinner*" (19:7).

It is beautiful to notice the gradation pointed by the Holy Spirit in the last three passages quoted above. In 7:34 Christ is simply "The *Friend* of publicans and sinners." In 15:2 it was said, "This Man *receiveth* sinners and eateth with them." But in 19:7 we are told, "He was gone to be *guest* with a man that is a sinner"! Thus did God make even the wrath of man to praise Him.

5. The Lord is here portrayed as a Man of Prayer.

It is indeed striking to see how often the Saviour is seen engaged in prayer in this Gospel. The following passages bring this out: "Now when all the people were baptized, it came to pass that *Jesus* also being baptized, *and praying,* the heaven was opened" (3:21). "And He withdrew Himself into the wilderness, and *prayed*" (5:16). "And it came to pass in those days, that He went out into a mountain *to pray,* and continued all night *in prayer* to God" (6:12). "And it came to pass about an eight days after these sayings, He took Peter and John and James, and went up into a mountain *to pray.* And *as He prayed,* the fashion of His countenance was altered" (9:28, 29). "And it came to pass, that, as He was *praying* in a certain place, when He ceased, one of His disciples said unto Him, Lord, teach us to pray" (11:1). "And the Lord said, Simon, Simon, behold, Satan hath desired to have you, that he may sift you as wheat: But I have *prayed* for thee, that thy faith fail not" (22:31, 32). "And He was withdrawn from them about a stone's cast, and kneeled down, and *prayed.* * * And being in an agony He *prayed* more earnestly" (22:41, 44). "Then said Jesus, Father, forgive them for they know not what they do" (23:34): only here do we find Him praying thus for His murderers. Add to these examples the fact that Luke alone records our Lord's teaching on Prayer which is found in 11:5-8, that he only tells us of His parable on Importunity in prayer (18:1-7), and that he alone tells us of the two men who went up to the Temple to pray, and it will be seen what a prominent place prayer has in Luke's Gospel.

6. Christ is frequently seen here Eating food.

"And one of the Pharisees desired Him that He

would eat with him. And He went into the Pharisee's house, and *sat down to meat*" (7:36). "And as He spake, a certain Pharisee besought Him to dine with him: and He went in, and *sat down to meat*" (11:37). "And it came to pass, as He went into the house of one of the chief Pharisees *to eat bread* on the Sabbath day, they watched Him" (14:1). "And when they saw it, they all murmured, saying, That He was gone *to be guest* with a man that is a sinner" (19:7). "And it came to pass, *as He sat at meat* with them, He took bread, and blessed it, and brake, and gave to them" (24:30). "And they gave Him a piece of a broiled fish, and of an honeycomb. And He took it, *and did eat* before them" (24:42, 43). It scarcely needs to be pointed out that these examples demonstrated the reality of His Manhood.

7. The Circumstances connected with His Death and Resurrection.

The awful hour spent in Gethsemane is described in this third Gospel with a fullness of detail which is not found in the others. Luke is the only one that tells us, "And there appeared an angel unto Him from heaven, *strengthening Him;*" as he is the only one to say, "And being in an agony He prayed more earnestly: and His sweat was as it were great drops of blood falling down to the ground" (22:43, 44). Then followed the Arrest, and as they were all leaving the Garden, we read, "And one of them smote the servant of the high priest, and cut off his ear. And Jesus answered and said, Suffer ye thus far, *and He touched his ear, and healed him*" (22: 50, 51). The other Evangelists record this incident of the smiting of the high priest's servant, but only

WHY FOUR GOSPELS? 129

Luke shows us the tenderness of the Saviour, full of compassion toward the suffering of others, right to the last.

Luke is the only one to tell us, "And there followed Him a great company of people, and of women, which also *bewailed* and *lamented* Him. But Jesus turning unto them said, Daughters of Jerusalem, weep not for Me, but weep for yourselves, and for your children" (23:27, 28). Appropriately, does this find a place here, bringing out, as it does, human emotions and sympathies. Luke is the only one to designate the place where the Saviour was crucified by its *Gentile* name—"And when they were come to the place, which is called *Calvary,* there they crucified Him" (23:33). And, again, Luke tells us, "A superscription also was written over Him in letters of *Greek, and Latin, and Hebrew,* This is the King of the Jews" (23:38). How this hints at the international scope of this third Gospel! Matthew and Mark give no hint of the "superscription" being written in the world-languages of the day; though John does, for he, again, presents Christ in connection with "the world." Luke is the only one to describe the conversion of the dying robber, and to record his witness to the *Human* perfections of the Lord Jesus: *"This Man* hath done nothing amiss" (23:41). So, too, it is only here we find a similar testimony borne by the Roman centurion: "Now when the centurion saw what was done, he glorified God, saying, Certainly this was *a righteous Man"* (23:47).

After His resurrection from the dead, it is only Luke who mentions that long walk of the Saviour with the two disciples, and of the familiar intercourse which they had together as they journeyed to

Emmaus. And Luke is the only one who presents the Lord to our view as eating food after He had risen in triumph from the grave.

It only remains to add a brief word concerning the characteristic manner in which this third Gospel closes. Luke alone tells us, "And He led them out as far as to Bethany, and *He lifted up His hands, and blessed them*" (24:50)—a beautiful touch is this! Then we are told, "And it came to pass, while He blessed them, He was parted from them, *and carried up into Heaven*" (24:51). Note, particularly, that Luke says that the Son of Man was "carried up into Heaven," not that He *ascended!* And then the curtain falls to the strains of the expressions of human joy and praise: "And they worshipped Him, and returned to Jerusalem *with great joy:* and were continually in the Temple, *praising* and blessing God. Amen" (24:52, 53).

THE GOSPEL OF JOHN.

THE GOSPEL OF JOHN.

AS we turn to the fourth Gospel we come to entirely different ground from that which we have traversed in the other three. True, the period of time which is covered by it, is the same as in the others; true, that some of the incidents that have already been looked at will here come before us again; and true it is that He who has occupied the central position in the narratives of the first three Evangelists, is the same One that is made preeminent by John; but otherwise, everything here is entirely new. The fourth Gospel is more elevated in its tone, its viewpoint is more exalted, its contents bring before us spiritual relationships rather than human ties, and higher glories are revealed as touching the peerless person of the Saviour. In each of the first three Gospels, Christ is viewed in human connections, but not so in the fourth. Matthew presents Him as the Son of David; Mark, as the perfect Workman of God; Luke, as the Son of Man; but John unveils His *Divine* glories. Again; Matthew writes, particularly, for the Jews; Mark, is specially adapted to God's servants; Luke's is written for men as men; but John's Gospel is concerned with the Family of God.

John's Gospel is the fourth book of the New Testament, and four is $3+1$. The numerals of Scripture are not employed fortuitously, but are used with Divine discrimination and significance. The reverent student is not left free to juggle with them at his own caprice, nor may he give to them an arbitrary meaning, so as to fit in with any private interpretations of his own. If he is honest, he will gather his definitions from the manner in which they are employed in Scripture itself. Thus, whether our statement that four is $3+1$ is an arbitrary assertion or not, must be determined by its support, or lack of it, in the Word. The numeral four is used two ways in the Bible. First, its meaning as a *whole* number, and second, its meaning as a *distributive* number. In its first usage, four is the world number, the number of the earth and all things therein, the number of the creature, as such; and hence, it comes to signify, Universality. But in its second usage, the distributive, when employed in connection with *a series,* it is frequently divided into three and one. Four is rarely, if ever an intensified two; that is, its significance does not represent 2×2.

The last paragraph sounds somewhat academical, we fear, but its force may become more apparent as we apply its principles to our present subject. The four Gospels form *a series,* and the character of their contents obviously divide them into a three and a one, just as in the four kinds of soil in the parable of the Sower, representing four classes of hearers of the Word, are *a series,* and similarly divided—three barren, and one fruitful. As we have seen, the first three Gospels have that in common which, necessarily, binds them together—each looking at Christ in *human* connections. But the fourth is clearly distinguished from the others by presenting Christ in a *Divine* relationship, and therefore it stands separated from the others. This conclusion is established beyond all doubt, when we observe that the character of its contents is in perfect accord with the significance of the numeral one. *One* speaks, primarily, of *God:* "Hear, O Israel: the Lord our God is *one* Lord" (Deut. 6:4). And again: "And the Lord shall be King over all the earth: in that day shall there be *one* Lord, and His name *one*" (Zech. 14:9). In all languages one is the symbol of *unity:* it excludes all others. The *first* of the ten commandments, therefore, was: "Thou shalt have *no other gods* before Me" (Ex. 20:3). So in John's Gospel, *the one* following the other three, it is *the Godhead* of Christ which is in view.

Each book in the Bible has a prominent and dominant theme which is peculiar to itself. Just as each member in the human body has its own particular function, so every book in the living Body of Divine Truth has its own special purpose and mission. The theme of John's Gospel is the Deity of Christ. Here, as nowhere else so fully, the Godhood of the Lord Jesus is presented to our view. That which is outstanding in this fourth Gospel is the Divine Sonship of our Saviour. In this Gospel we are shown that the One born at Bethlehem, who walked this earth for over thirty years, who was crucified at Calvary, and who forty-three days later departed from these scenes, was none other than "the Only-Begotten of the Father." The evidence presented for this is overwhelming, the proofs almost without number, and the effect of contemplating them must be to bow our hearts in worship before "The great God, and our Saviour Jesus Christ" (Titus 2:13).

Here is a theme worthy of our most reverent and prayerful attention. If such Divine care was taken, as we saw in the previous chapter, to guard the perfections of our Lord's humanity, equally so, has the Holy Spirit seen to it that there should be no uncertainty concerning the affirmation of the absolute Deity of our Saviour. Just as the Old Testament prophets made known that the Coming One should be a Man, and a perfect Man, so did Messianic prediction also give plain intimation that He would be *more* than a Man. Through Isaiah, God foretold that unto Israel a Child should be born, and unto them a Son should be given, and that "the government shall be upon His shoulder: and His name shall be called Wonderful, Counsellor, *The mighty God,* the Father of the ages (Heb.), the Prince of Peace" (9:6). Through Micah, He declared, "But thou, Bethlehem Ephratah, though thou be little among the thousands of Judah, yet out of thee shall He come forth unto Me that is to be Ruler in Israel: whose goings forth have been *from the days of eternity"*—marginal rendering (5: 2)! Through Zechariah, He said "Awake, O Sword, against My Shepherd, and against the Man that is *My Fellow,* saith the Lord of hosts" (13:7). Through the Psalmist, He announced, "The Lord said *unto my Lord,* Sit Thou at My right hand, until I make Thine enemies Thy footstool" (110:1). And again, when looking forward to the time of the second Advent, "The Lord hath said unto Me, *Thou art My Son;* this day have I begotten Thee" (or, "brought Thee forth") 2:7.

Coming now to the New Testament we may single out two or three of the most explicit witnesses to the Deity of Christ. In Rom. 9, where the apostle is enumerating the peculiar privileges of Israel, he says in verse 5, "Whose are the fathers, and of whom as concerning the flesh Christ came, who is over all, *God* blessed for ever. Amen." In 1 Cor. 15 we are told, "And the first man is of the earth, earthy, but the second Man *is the Lord from Heav-*

WHY FOUR GOSPELS?

en" (v. 47). In Col. 1:16 we read, "For *by Him were all things created,* that are in heaven, and that are in earth, visible and invisible, whether they be thrones, or dominions, or principalities or powers: all things were created *by Him and for Him;*" and again, in 2:9, "For in Him dwelleth *all the fullness of the Godhead* bodily." In Heb. 1 we learn that "God, who at sundry times and in divers manners spake in time past unto the fathers by the prophets, Hath in these last days spoken unto us by His Son, whom He hath appointed Heir of all things, by whom also He made the worlds; Who being *the Brightness of His glory, and the express Image of His person,* and upholding all things by the Word of His power, when He had by Himself purged our sins, sat down on the right hand of the Majesty on high" (Heb. 1:1-3). While in Rev. 19:16 we are informed that when He comes back to earth again, "He hath on His vesture and on His thigh a name written, *King of kings, and Lord of lords.*" A more emphatic, positive, and unequivocal testimony to the absolute Deity of Christ could not be borne.

In these days of widespread departure from the Truth, it cannot be insisted upon too strongly or too frequently that the Lord Jesus Christ is none other than the Second Person in the Holy Trinity. Vicious but specious are the attacks now being made upon this cardinal article in the faith once for all delivered to the saints. Satan, who poses as an angel of light, is now sending forth his ministers "transformed as the ministers of righteousness." Men who are loudly trumpeting their faith in the verbal inspiration of Scripture, and who even profess to believe in the vicarious Sacrifice of Christ are, nevertheless, denying the absolute Godhood of Him whom they claim to be serving: they repudiate His essential Deity, they deny His Eternality, and reduce Him to the level of a mere creature. It was concerning men of this class that the Holy Spirit said, "For such are false apostles, *deceitful workers*, transforming themselves into the apostles of Christ" (2 Cor. 11:13).

In keeping with the special theme of the fourth Gospel, it is here that we have the fullest unveiling of Christ's Divine glories. It is here we behold Him dwelling "with God" before time began and before ever a creature was formed (1:1, 2). It is here that He is denominated "the Only Begotten of the Father" (1:14). It is here John the Baptist bears record that "this is the Son of God" (1:34). It is here we read, "This beginning of miracles did Jesus in Cana of Galilee, and *manifested forth His glory*" (2:11). It is here we are told that the Saviour said, "Destroy this temple, and in three days *I will raise it up*" (2:19). It is here we read that God sent His Son into the world, not to condemn but to save (3:17). It is here we are told, "The Father loveth the Son, and hath given all things into His hands" (3:35). It is here we learn that Christ declared, "For as the Father raiseth up the dead, and quickeneth them; *even so the Son* quickeneth whom He will. For the Father judgeth no man, but hath committed all judgment unto the Son: That all men should honor the Son, *even as they honor the Father*. He that honoreth not the Son honoreth not the Father which hath sent Him" (5:21-23). It is here that we find Him affirming, "For the Bread of God is He *which cometh down from Heaven,* and giveth life unto the world" (6:35). It is here we find Him saying, "Before Abraham was, I am" (8:58). It is here that we find Him declaring, "I and Father *are One*" (10:30). It is here we hear Him saying, "He that hath seen Me, hath seen the Father" (14:9). It is here He promises, "Whatsoever ye shall ask in My name, that will I do, that the Father may be glorified in the Son" (14:13). It is here that He asks, "And now, O Father, glorify Thou Me with Thine own Self with the glory which I had with Thee *before the world was*" (17:5).

Before we take up John's Gospel in detail, and examine some of the more prominent lines in his delineation of Christ's person and ministry, a few words should be said concerning the *dispensational* scope and bearings of this Gospel. It should be evident at once that this one is quite different from the other Gospels. There, Christ is seen in a human relationship, and as connected with an earthly people; but here, He is viewed in a Divine relationship, and as connected with a heavenly people. It is true that the mystery of the one Body is not unfolded here, rather is it the *family* of God which is in view. It is also true that the Heavenly Calling is not fully disclosed, yet are there plain intimations of it— what else can be said, for example of the Lord's words which are found in 14:2, 3?—"In My Father's House are many mansions: if it were not so, I would have told you. I go to prepare a place for you. And if I go and prepare a place for you, I will come again, and receive you unto Myself; *that where I am, there ye may be also.*"

In the first three Gospels, Christ is seen connected with the Jews, proclaiming the Messianic kingdom, a proclamation which ceased, however, as soon as it became evident that the Nation had rejected Him. But here, in John's Gospel, His rejection is announced at the beginning, for in the very first chapter we are told, "He came unto His own, and His own received Him not." It is, therefore, most significant to note that John's Gospel, which instead of presenting Christ in connection with Israel, views Him as related to believers by spiritual ties, was not written until *after* A. D. 70, when the Temple was destroyed, and the Jews dispersed throughout the world!

The dispensational limitations which attach to much that is found in the first three Gospels, do not hold good with John's Gospel, for as Son of God, He can be known only by believers as such. On *this* plane the Jew has no priority. The Jews' claim upon Christ was purely a fleshly one, whereas believers are related to the Son of God by *spiritual* union. The Son of David, and the Son of Man titles link Christ to the earth, but the "Son of God" connects Him with the Father in Heaven; hence, in this fourth Gospel, the earthly kingdom is almost entirely ignored. In harmony with these facts we may observe, that it is only here in John's Gospel we hear of Christ saying, "And *other* sheep I have, which are not of *this* (i. e., the Jewish) fold. Them also I must bring, and they shall hear My voice; and there shall be *one fold* (i. e., the Christian fold), and one Shepherd" (10:16). It is only here in John we learn of the wider scope of God's purpose in the Death of His Son, "Being high priest that year, he prophesied that Jesus should die for that nation; And not for that nation only, but that also He should gather together in one the children of God that were scattered abroad" (11:51, 52). It is only here in John that we have fully unfolded the relation of the Holy Spirit to believers. And it is only

WHY FOUR GOSPELS?

here in John that we have recorded our Lord's High Priestly prayer, which gives a sample of His *present* intercession on high. These considerations, then, should make it abundantly clear that the *dispensational bearings* of John's Gospel are entirely different from the other three.

Coming now to a closer view of this fourth Gospel we may observe how striking are its opening verses: "In the beginning was the Word, and the Word was with God, and the Word was God. The same was in the beginning with God. All things were made by Him; and without Him was not anything made that was made" (1:1-3). How entirely different is this from what we find in the introductory statements in the other Gospels! John starts, immediately, by presenting Christ as the Son of God, not as the Son of David, or the Son of Man. John takes us back to the beginning, and shows that our Lord had no beginning, for He was *in the beginning*. John goes right back behind creation, and shows that Christ was Himself the Creator.

Every clause in these opening verses is worthy of our closest attention. First, the Lord Jesus is here termed, "The *Word*." The significance of this title may, perhaps, be most easily grasped by comparing with it what is said in v. 18 of this first chapter of John. Here we are told: "No man hath seen God at any time; the Only Begotten Son, which is in the bosom of the Father, He hath *declared* Him," or "told Him out." Christ is the One who came here to tell out God. He came here to make God intelligible to men. As we read in Heb. 1: "God, who at sundry times and in divers manners *spake* in time past unto the fathers by the prophets, Hath in these last days *spoken unto us by His Son*." Christ is the final Spokesman of God. Again; the force of this title of Christ, "the Word," may be discovered by comparing it with the name given to the Bible—the Word of God. What are the Scriptures? They are, the *Word* of God. And what does that mean? This: that the Scriptures reveal God's mind, express His will, make known His perfections, and lay bare His heart. This is precisely what the Lord Jesus Christ has done for the Father. But let us enter a little more into detail:

(a) A "word" is *a medium of manifestation.* I have in my mind a thought, but others know not its nature. But the moment I clothe that thought in words, it becomes cognizable. Words, then, make objective, unseen thoughts. This is precisely what the Lord Jesus has done, as the "Word" Christ has made manifest the invisible God. Christ is God clothed in perfect humanity.

(b) A "word" is a *means of communication.* By means of words I transmit information to others. By words I express myself, make known my will, and impart knowledge. So, Christ as the "Word," is the Divine Transmitter, communicating to us the Life and Love of God.

(c) A "word" is a *method of revelation.* By his words a speaker reveals both his intellectual caliber and his moral character. It is by our words we shall be justified, and by our words we shall be condemned. And Christ, as the "Word," fully reveals the attributes and the character of God. How fully He has revealed God! He has displayed His power: He has manifested His wisdom: He has exhibited His holiness: He has made known His grace: He

WHY FOUR GOSPELS? 143

has unveiled His heart. In Christ, and nowhere else, is God fully and finally revealed.

But was not God fully revealed in Nature? "Revealed," yes; but "fully revealed," no. Nature conceals as well as reveals. Nature is under the Curse, and is far different now from what it was in the day that it left the hands of the Creator. Nature is imperfect to day, and how can that which is imperfect be a perfect medium for manifesting the infinite perfections of God. The ancients had Nature before them, and what did they learn of God? Let that altar, which the apostle beheld in one of the great centers of ancient culture and learning, make answer—"To the *unknown God,*" is what he found inscribed thereon. No; in Christ, and in and by Him alone, is God fully and finally revealed.

But lest this figurative expression—"the Word"—should convey to us an inadequate conception of the Divine person of the Lord Jesus, the Holy Spirit goes on to say, in the opening verse of this Gospel, "And the Word *was with God.*" This denotes His separate Personality, and also indicates His essential relation to the Godhead. He was not *"in* God," as an Ideal in His mind, but He was *"with* God." And, as though this were not strong enough, the Spirit expressly adds, "And the Word *was God.*" Not an emanation from God, but none other than God. Not merely a manifestation of God, but God Himself made manifest. Not only the Revealer of God, but God Himself revealed. A more unequivocal affirmation of the essential Deity of the Lord Jesus Christ it is impossible to imagine. Granted, that we are in the realm of mystery, yet, the force of what is here affirmed of the absolute Godhead of Christ cannot be honestly evaded. As to *how* Christ can be the Revealer of God, and yet God Himself revealed; as to how He can be "with God," and yet be God, are high mysteries that our finite minds are no more capable of fathoming than we can understand how that God can be without beginning. What is here stated in John 1:1, is to be received by simple, unquestioning faith.

Next we read, "All things were made by Him; and without Him (apart from Him) was not anything made that was made" (1:3). Here, again, the absolute Deity of Christ is emphatically affirmed, for Creation is ascribed to Him, and none but God can create. Man, despite all his proud boasts and lofty pretentions, is utterly unable to create even a blade of grass. If, then, Christ is the Creator, He must be *God*. Observe, too, that the *whole* of Creation is here attributed to the Son of God—*"all* things were made by Him." This would not be true, if He were Himself a creature, even though the first and highest. But nothing is excepted—*"all* things were made by Him." Just as He was Eternal—before all things—so was He the Originator of all things.

Again we are told, "In Him was *life;* and the life was the Light of men." This follows, necessarily, from what has been said in the previous verse. If Christ created all things, He must be the Fount of *life*. He is the Life-Giver. But more: "The Life was the *light* of men." What this means is made clear in the verses that follow. "There was *a man* (in contrast from "the Word," who is *God*) sent from God, whose name was John," and he, "Came for a witness, to bear witness of the Light, that all through him might believe" (1:6, 7). Compare with these words what we are told in 1 John 1:5,

"God is Light, and in Him is no darkness at all." The conclusion, then, is irresistible, that the Lord Jesus is none other than God, the Second Person in the Holy Trinity.

But we pass now to the fourteenth verse of this opening chapter of John. Having shown the relation of our Lord to Time—without beginning; having declared His relation to the Godhead—a separate Person of the Trinity, but Himself also God; having defined His relation to the Universe—the Creator of it, and the great Life-Giver; having stated His relation to Men—the One who is their God, their "Light," having announced that the Baptist bore witness to Him as the Light; and having described the reception which He met with here upon earth—unknown by the world, rejected by Israel, but received by a people who were "born of God," the Holy Spirit goes on to say, "And the Word was made (better, "became") flesh, and dwelt (tabernacled) among us, and we beheld His glory, the glory as of the Only Begotten of the Father, full of grace and truth." This verse announces the Divine incarnation, and brings out, once more, the Divine glories of the One born of Mary.

"The Word became flesh." He became what He was not previously. He did not cease to be God, but He became Man. Becoming Man, He "tabernacled" among men. He pitched His tent here for thirty-three years. And then we are told that the testimony of those whose eyes Divine power had opened, was, "we beheld *His glory.*" The language of this verse takes us back in thought to the Tabernacle which was pitched in the wilderness, of old. The Tabernacle was the place of Jehovah's abode in the midst of Israel. It was there that He made His dwelling-place.

The Tabernacle was where God met with His people, hence was it termed "the Tent of Meeting." There, within the Holy of Holies was the Shekinah Glory manifested. The Lord Jesus Christ was the Antitype. He was, in His own person, the Meeting-place between God and men. And just as the Shekinah—the visible and glorious manifestation of Jehovah—was seen in the Holy of Holies, so those who came near to Christ, in faith, "beheld *His glory*." The Lord Jesus was God manifest in the flesh, displaying "the glory as of the Only Begotten of the Father." For, as the 18th verse goes on to say, "No man hath seen God at any time; the Only Begotten Son, which is in the bosom of the Father, *He hath declared Him*." Thus, the essential Deity of the One born at Bethlehem is, once more, expressly affirmed.

Next we have the witness of John the Baptist. This is quite different from what we find in the other Gospels. Here there is no Call to Repentance, there is no announcement of "The kingdom of heaven" being at hand, and there is no mention of Christ Himself being baptized by His forerunner. Instead of these things, here we find John saying, "Behold *the Lamb of God,* which taketh away the sin of the world" (1:29). And again he says, "And I saw, and bare record that this is *the Son of God*" (1:34). It is also to be noted that when referring to the anointing of Christ with the Holy Spirit, a word is used which is not found in the other Gospels: "And John bare record, saying, I saw the Spirit descending from Heaven like a dove, and it *abode* upon Him" (1:32). The Spirit did not come upon Him and then leave again, as with the prophets of old: it "abode," a characteristic and prominent word in John's Gospel (see particularly chapter 15), having to do with the *Divine* side of things, and speaking of Fellowship. We have the same word again in 14:10—"Believest thou not that I am in the Father, and the Father in Me? the words that I speak unto you I speak not of Myself: but the Father that dwelleth (*"abideth,"* it should be) in Me, He doeth the works."

The first chapter closes by describing the personal Call (not the *ministerial* call as in the other Gospels) of the first disciples of the Lord. Here only do we read of Christ saying to Nathaniel, "Before that Philip called thee, when thou wast under the fig tree, *I saw thee*" (1:48): thus manifesting His Omniscience. Here only do we find recorded Nathaniel's witness to Christ. "Rabbi, Thou art *the Son of God;* Thou art the King of Israel" (1:49). And here only did Christ tell His disciples that, in the coming Day they should "see Heaven open, and the angels of God ascending and descending on the Son of Man" (1:51).

Coming now to the second chapter, we find described there the first miracle performed by the Lord Jesus, namely, the turning of the water into wine. John alone records this, for only *God* can fill the human heart with that Divine joy, of which the wine was here the emblem. In this miracle we are shown the *"Word"* at work. He, Himself, *did* nothing. He simply told the servants what to do, and at His word the wonder was performed. The special point in connection with this miracle is stated in v. 11, "This beginning of miracles did Jesus in Cana of Galilee, and *manifested forth His glory;* and His disciples believed on Him."

In the remainder of this chapter we witness Christ cleansing the Temple. Here, again, John brings into the picture his own distinctive lines. Here only do we find the Lord terming the Temple *"My Father's house"* (v. 16). Here only do we find Him saying, in reply to the challenge of His critics for a sign, "Destroy this temple (meaning His body), and in three days *I will raise it up"* (v. 19). And, here only do we read, "Now when He was in Jerusalem at the Passover, in the feast, many believed in His name, when they saw the miracles which He did. But Jesus did not commit Himself unto them, *because He knew all,* and needed not that any should testify of man: *for He knew what was in man"* (vv. 23-25). What a proof was this of His Deity! Only *He* "knew what was in man." Compare with this the words of 1 Kings 8:39—"Hear Thou in Heaven Thy dwelling place, and forgive, and do, and give to every man according to his ways, whose heart Thou knowest—*for Thou, even Thou only,* knowest the hearts of all the children of men." In thus reading the hearts of men, what a demonstration did the Saviour give, that He was God manifest in flesh!

John 3 records the interview of Nicodemus with Christ—something not found in the other three Gospels. In full accord with the scope of this Gospel, we find the Saviour here speaking to Nicodemus not of faith or repentance, but of the New Birth, which is the *Divine* side in salvation, declaring that, "Except a man be born again, he cannot see the kingdom of God." And only here in the four Gospels do we read, *"God* so loved the world, that He gave *His Only Begotten Son,* that whosoever believeth in Him should not perish, but have everlasting life" (3:16).

In John 4 we find another incident that is not

described elsewhere, namely, the Lord's dealings with the poor Samaritan adulteress. And here, once more, we behold flashes of His Divine glory shining forth. He tells her, "Whosoever drinketh of the water that I shall give him shall never thirst; but the water that I shall give him shall be in him a well of water springing up into everlasting life" (v. 14). He manifests His omniscience by declaring, "Thou hast had five husbands; and he whom thou now hast is not thy husband" (v. 18). He speaks to her of worshipping the Father "in spirit and in truth." He reveals Himself to her as the great "I am" (v. 26). He brings her from death unto life, and out of darkness into His own marvellous light. Finally, He proved His *oneness* with the Father by affirming, "My meat is to do the will of Him that sent Me, and to finish His work" (4:34).

John 5 opens by recording the healing of the impotent man who had an infirmity thirty-eight years. None of the other Evangelists make mention of it. This miracle evidenced "the *Word*" at work again. He does nothing to the poor sufferer, not even laying hands upon him. He simply speaks the authoritative and healing word, "Rise, take up thy bed, and walk," and "immediately," we read, "the man was made whole, and took up his bed, and walked" (v. 9). The miracle was performed on the Sabbath day, and the Lord's enemies used this as an occasion of criticism. Not only so, but we read, "Therefore did the Jews persecute Jesus, and sought to slay Him, because He had done these things on the Sabbath day" (v. 16). We also read in the other Gospels, of Christ being condemned because He transgressed the Jews' traditions respecting the Sabbath. But there, we find a very different reply from

Him than what is recorded here. There, He insisted on the right of performing works of mercy on the Sabbath. There, too, He appealed to the priests carrying out their Temple duties on the Sabbath. But here He takes higher ground. Here, He says, "My Father worketh hitherto, *and I work*" (v. 17). The meaning of these words could not be mistaken. Christ reminded His critics, how that His "Father" worked on the Sabbath day, worked in connection with His government of the universe, in maintaining the orderly course of Nature, in sending rain, and so on. And because *He* was *one* with "the Father," He insisted that what was right for the Father to do, was equally right for Him to do. That this was the force of His reply, is clear from the next verse, "Therefore the Jews sought the more to kill Him, because He not only had broken the Sabbath, but said also that God was His Father, *making Himself equal with God*" (5:18). In the remaining verses of the chapter we find that Christ continued to affirm His absolute equality with the Father.

The sixth chapter opens by describing a miracle, which is narrated by each of the other Evangelists, the Feeding of the five thousand. But, here, it is followed by a lengthy discourse which is not recorded elsewhere. Here the Lord presents Himself as "The Bread of God," which had come down from Heaven to give life unto the world. He here declares that He alone can satisfy the needy soul of man: "And Jesus said unto them, I am the Bread of Life: he that cometh to Me shall never hunger; and he that believeth on Me shall never thirst" (v. 35). We cannot now follow the details of this wonderful chapter, but it will be evident to the student

WHY FOUR GOSPELS? 151

that it is the *Divine* side of things which is here dwelt upon. For example: it is here we are told that the Saviour said, "No man can come to Me, except *the Father* which hath sent Me *draw him*" (v. 44). It is here we are told that "Jesus *knew* from the beginning who they were that believed not, and who should betray Him" (v. 64). And it is here we learn that when many of the disciples "went back and walked no more with Him," and He said to the twelve, "Will ye also go away?" that Peter replied, "Lord, to whom shall we go? *Thou hast the words of eternal life*" (v. 68).

The seventh chapter brings before us Christ at Jerusalem during the feast of tabernacles. There is much here that is of deepest interest, but it is beside our present purpose to give a complete exposition. We are not here writing a brief commentary on John, rather are we attempting to point out that which is distinctive and characteristic in this fourth Gospel. Notice, then, one or two lines in this scene which serve to emphasize the Divine glories of Christ. We are told that, about the middle of the feast, "Jesus went up into the Temple, and taught." His teaching must have been exceedingly impressive, for we read, "And the Jews *marvelled,* saying, How knoweth this man letters, having never learned" (v. 15). But, arresting as was His manner of delivery, what He said only served to bring out the enmity of those who heard Him: "Then they sought to take Him: but no man laid hands on Him, because His hour was not yet come" (v. 30). How striking this is, and how thoroughly in accord with the central theme of John's Gospel! bringing out, as it does, the *Divine* side, by showing us God's complete control over the enemies of His Son. Next, we read "In the last day, that great day of the feast, Jesus stood and cried, saying, If any man thirst, let him come unto Me, and drink. He that believeth on Me, as the Scripture hath said, out of his belly shall flow rivers of living water" (vv. 37, 38). How this brings out the Divine sufficiency of Christ! None but God could make such a claim as that. Finally, we may observe here, that when the Pharisees heard that many of the people believed on Him, they "sent officers to take Him" (vv. 31, 32). How striking was the sequel: "Then came the officers to the chief priests and Pharisees; and they said unto them, Why have ye not brought Him? The officers answered, *Never man spake like this Man*" (vv. 45, 46).

John 8 opens by recording the incident of the woman taken in adultery, brought to Christ by the scribes and Pharisees. Their motive in doing this was an evil one. It was not that they were zealous of upholding the claims of God's law, but that they sought to ensnare God's Son. They set a trap for Him. They reminded Him that Moses had given commandment that such as this woman should be stoned—"but what sayest *Thou?*" they asked. He had declared that, "God sent not His Son into the world to condemn the world; but that the world through Him might be saved" (John 3:17). Would He, then, suffer this guilty adulteress to escape the penalty of the Law? If so, what became of His other claim, "Think not that I am come to destroy the Law, or the prophets: I am not come to destroy, *but to fulfil*" (Matt. 5:17)? It seemed as though He was caught on the horns of a dilemma. If He gave the word for her to be stoned, where was *grace?* On the other hand, if He allowed her to go free, where was *righteousness?* Ah, how blessedly did His Divine wisdom appear, in the masterly manner in which He dealt with the situation. Said He to them that sought to trap Him, "He that is without sin among you, let him first cast a stone at her." It was "the *Word*" at work again, the *Divine* Word, for we read, "And they which heard Him, *being convicted by their conscience,* went out one by one, beginning at the eldest, even unto the last: and Jesus was left alone, and the woman standing in the midst" (v. 9). The way was now open for Him to display His mercy. The Law required two "witnesses" at least; but none were left. To the woman He said, "Where are those thine accusers? hath no man condemned thee?" And she answered, "No man, Lord." And then, to manifest His holiness He said, "Neither do I condemn thee: go, *and sin no more*" (v. 11). Thus, do we here behold His glory, "the glory as of the Only Begotten of the Father, *full of grace and truth.*" Then followed that lovely discourse in which Christ proclaimed Himself as "The Light of the world," saying, "he that followeth Me shall not walk in darkness, but shall have the light of life" (v. 12). This was peculiarly appropriate to the occasion, for He had just given proof that He *was* such, by turning the searching Light of God upon the conscience of those who accused the adulteress.

What follows in the next chapter is closely linked to that which has just been before us. Here Christ gives sight to a man who had been blind from his birth, and immediately before He gives light to the darkened eyes of this man, He uses the occasion to say, again, "As long as I am in the world, I am the light of the world" (9:5). The sequel to this miracle had both its pathetic and its blessed sides. The one who had had his eyes opened was brought to the Pharisees, and after a lengthy examination they excommunicated him, because of the bold testimony he had borne to his Benefactor. But we are told, "Jesus heard that they had cast him out; and when He had found Him, He said unto him, Dost thou believe on the Son of God? And he answered and said, Who is he, Lord, that I might believe on Him? And Jesus said unto him, Thou hast both seen Him, and He it is that talketh with thee. And he said, Lord, I believe. And he worshipped Him" (vv. 35-37). Thus did Christ graciously evidence that when God begins a good work in a soul, He ceases not until it has been perfected. The chapter closes with a most solemn word against those who opposed Christ, in which we behold the Light blinding: "And Jesus said, For judgment I am come into this world, that they which see not might see; and that they which see *might be made blind*" (v. 39).

John 10 is the chapter in which Christ is revealed as the Good Shepherd, and there is much in it which brings out His Divine glories. Here He presents Himself as the Owner of the fold, and makes it known that believers, under the figure of sheep, belong to Him. They are His property, as well as the objects of His tender solicitude. They know Him, and they are known of Him. His, is the Voice they follow, and the voice of strangers they heed not. For the sheep He will lay down His life. But, be it carefully noted, the Saviour declares, "No man taketh it from Me, but I lay it down of Myself. I have power to lay it down, and I have power to take it again" (v. 18). No mere man could have made good such a claim as this. Nor could any mere

WHY FOUR GOSPELS? 155

human teacher say to his disciples, "And I give unto them eternal life; and they shall never perish, neither shall any pluck them out of My hand" (v. 28). That He was *more* than Man, that He was God the Son, incarnate, is expressly affirmed in the words with which the Saviour here closed His discourse—"I and Father are one" (v. 30).

John 11 brings us to what, perhaps, was the most wonderful miracle that our Lord performed, while here on earth, namely, the Raising of Lazarus. Record of this was, appropriately, reserved for the fourth Gospel. The others tell us of the raising of the daughter of Jairus, just dead; and Luke mentions the raising of the widow of Nain's son, as his body was on the way to the cemetery; but John only records the raising of Lazarus, who had been in the grave four days, and whose body had already begun to corrupt. Signally did the performance of this miracle demonstrate Christ to be the Son of God. Here, too, we behold "the *Word*" at work. The daughter of Jairus He took by the hand; concerning the widow's son, we read, "He touched the bier;" but here He did nothing but *speak:* first, to the spectators to remove the stone which lay over the entrance to the grave, and then to Lazarus, He cried, "Come forth."

John 12 brings us to the close of our Lord's public ministry as it is followed in this Gospel. The chapter opens with a scene which has won the hearts of all who have gazed by faith upon it. The Saviour is seen in a Bethany home, where deep gratitude made Him a supper, and Lazarus is also one of the guests. After the meal was over, Mary anointed His feet with fragrant ointment that was "very costly," and wiped His feet with her hair. It is very striking to notice the differences between Matthew's account of this incident and what is recorded here. It is only John who tells us that Lazarus sat at the table with the Lord; it is only John who says that "Martha served," and it is only John who gives the name of this devoted woman who expressed such love for Christ: here everything is "made manifest" by the Light. Moreover, note particularly, that Matthew says the woman poured the ointment "on His head" (26:7), but here in John, we are told, she "anointed the feet of Jesus" (12:3). The two accounts are not contradictory, but supplementary. Both are true, but we see the hand of the Holy Spirit controlling each Evangelist to record only that which was in keeping with his theme. In Matthew it is the King who is before us, hence it is His *"head"* that is anointed; but in John we are shown the Son of God, and therefore does Mary here take her place at His *"feet"!*

John 13 is in striking contrast with what is found at the beginning of the previous chapter. There, we behold the feet of the Lord; here we see the feet of His disciples. There, we saw His feet *anointed;* here, the feet of the disciples are *washed.* There, the feet of Christ were anointed with *fragrant and costly ointment;* here the feet of the disciples are washed with *water.* There, the feet of the Lord was washed by another; but here, the feet of the disciples are washed by none other than the Son of God Himself. And observe that the anointing of His feet *comes before* the washing of the disciples' feet, for in all things He must have the pre-eminence. And what a contrast is here presented! The "feet" speak of the walk. The feet of the disciples were soiled: their walk needed to be cleansed. Not so with the

WHY FOUR GOSPELS?

Lord of glory: His walk emitted nought but a sweet fragrance to the Father.

At first sight it appears strange that this lowly task of washing the disciples' feet should be recorded by John. And yet the very fact that it is recorded *here* supplies the surest key to the interpretation of its significance. The act itself only brought out the amazing condescension of the Son of God, who would stoop so low as to perform the common duties of a slave. But the mention of this incident by John indicates there is a *spiritual* meaning to the act. And such, indeed, there was. The "feet," as we have seen, point to the walk, and "water" is the well known emblem of the written Word. Spiritually, the act spoke of Christ maintaining the walk of His disciples, removing the defilements which unfit them for communion with a holy God. It was members of His Church that were here being cleansed by the Head "with the washing of water by the Word" (Eph. 5:26). How fitting, then, that this should have found a place in this fourth Gospel, for who but a *Divine Person* is capable of cleansing the walk of believers and maintaining their fellowship with the Father!

In the remainder of John 13 and to the end of chapter 16 we have what is known as the Lord's "Pascal discourse." This, too, is peculiar to John, and almost everything in it brings out the Divine glories of the Saviour. It is here that He says to the disciples, "Ye call Me Master and Lord: and ye say well; *for so I am*" (13:13). It is here that Christ said, anticipating the Cross, "Now is the Son of Man *glorified,* and God is glorified in Him" (13:31). It is here that He speaks of going away to "prepare a place" for His people (14:2, 3). It is here He invites His disciples to pray in His name (14:13). It is here He says, "Peace I leave with you, My peace I give unto you: not as the world giveth, give I unto you" (14:27). It is here that He says so much about fruit-bearing, under the beautiful figure of the Vine. It is here that He speaks of "The Comforter *whom I will send* unto you from the Father" (15:26). And it is here that He declares of the Holy Spirit, "He shall glorify *Me:* for He shall receive of *Mine,* and shall show it unto you" (16:14).

John 17 contains what is known as the High Priestly prayer of Christ. Nothing like it is found in the other Gospels. It gives us a specimen of His present ministry on High. Here we find the Saviour saying, "Father, the hour is come; *glorify Thy Son,* that Thy Son also may glorify Thee" (v. 1). Here He speaks of Himself as the One given "power over all flesh" (v. 2). Here He is inseparably linked with "the only true God" (v. 3). Here He speaks (by way of anticipation) of having "finished" the work given Him to do (v. 4). Here He asks, "O Father, glorify Thou Me with Thine own self with the glory which I had with Thee before the world was" (v. 5). Here He prays for His own beloved people: for their preservation from evil, for the supply of their every need, for their sanctification and unification. His perfect equality with the Father is evidenced when He says, "Father, *I will that* they also, whom Thou hast given Me, be with Me where I am; that they may behold My glory, which Thou hast given Me: for Thou lovest Me before the foundation of the world" (v. 24).

The remaining chapters will be considered in another connection, so we pass on now to notice some of the general features which characterize this Gospel in its parts and as a whole.

I. THINGS OMITTED FROM JOHN'S GOSPEL.

While examining the second Gospel, we dwelt at some length upon the different things of which Mark took no notice, and saw that the items excluded made manifest the perfections of his particular portrayal of Christ. Here, too, a similar line of thought may be followed out at even greater length. Much that is found in the first three Gospels is omitted by John, as being irrelevant to his special theme. Some of the more outstanding of these we shall now consider:

1. In John's Gospel there is *no genealogy,* neither His legal through Joseph, nor his personal through Mary. Nor is there any account of His *birth.* Instead, as we have seen, He was "In the beginning." For a similar reason, John is silent about Herod's attempt to slay the Christ Child, about the flight into Egypt, and subsequent return to Galilee. Nothing is said about the Lord Jesus as a Boy of twelve, in the midst of the doctors in the Temple. No reference is made to the years spent at Nazareth, and no hint is given of Christ working at the carpenter's bench before He began His public ministry. All these are passed over as not being germane.

2. Here, there is no description of His *baptism.* Mark refers to the Lord Jesus being baptized by his forerunner, and Matthew and Luke each describe at length the attendant circumstances. John's reason for saying nothing about this is obvious. In His baptism, Christ, in condescending grace, took His place alongside of His needy people, saying to the one who baptized Him, "Thus it becometh *us* to fulfill all righteousness" (Matt. 3:15).

3. John says nothing about *the Temptation*. Here, again, we may observe the superintending hand of the Holy Spirit, guiding the different Evangelists in the selection of their material. Each of the first three Gospels make mention of the season spent by Christ in the wilderness, where He was tempted for forty days of the Devil. But John is silent about it. And why? Because John is presenting Christ as God the Son, and "God *cannot* be tempted" (Jas. 1:13).

4. There is no account of *His Transfiguration*. At first sight this seems strange, but a little attention to details will reveal the reason for this. The wonderful scene witnessed by the three disciples upon the holy mount, was not an unveiling of His Divine glories, but a miniature representation, a spectacular showing forth of the Son of Man coming in His *kingdom* (see Matt. 16:28 etc.). But the *earthly* kingdom does not fall within the scope of this Gospel. Here, it is spiritual and heavenly relationships which are made most prominent.

5. Here there is *no Appointing of the Apostles*. In the other Gospels we find the Lord Jesus selecting, equipping, and sending forth the Twelve, to preach, and to heal; and in Luke we also read of Him sending out the Seventy. But here, in harmony with the character of this Gospel, all ministry and miracle working is left entirely in the hands of the Son of God.

6. Never once is Christ here seen *Praying*. This does not come out so clearly in our English translation as it does in the original Greek. In John's Gospel we never find the word associated with Christ

WHY FOUR GOSPELS?

which signifies taking the place of a supplicant; instead, the word "erotos" is used, and this word denotes "speaking" as to an equal. It is very striking to compare what each Evangelist records following the miracle of the Feeding of the five thousand: Matt. says, "And when He had sent the multitudes away, He went up into a mountain apart *to pray*" (14:23). Mark says, "When He had sent them away, He departed into a mountain *to pray*" (6:46). Luke also follows his narration of this miracle with the words, "And it came to pass, as He was alone *praying*" (9:18). But when we come to the fourth Gospel, we read, "He departed again into a mountain Himself alone" (6:15), and *there John stops!*

The contents of John 17 may seem to contradict what we have just said above, but really it is not so. At the beginning of the chapter we read, "Jesus lifted up His eyes to Heaven, *and said,* Father, the hour is come; glorify Thy Son, that Thy Son also may glorify Thee" (v. 1). And at its close we read that He said, "Father *I will* that they also, whom Thou hast given Me, be with Me where I am" (v. 24). Thus He spoke to the Father *as to an Equal.*

7. We never read in John's Gospel of *"The Coming of the Son of Man,"* and for the same reason as this, He is never addressed as "The Son of David" here. The Coming of the Son of Man always has reference to His return to the earth itself, coming back to His earthly people. But here we read, not of a restored Palestine, but of the "Father's House" and its "many mansions," of Christ going on High to prepare a place "for His heavenly people, and of Him coming back to receive them unto Himself, that there may they be also.

8. We never find the word *"Repent"* in John. In the other Gospels this is a term of frequent occurrence; what, then, is the reason for its absence here? In the other Gospels the sinner is viewed as *guilty*, and needing, therefore, to "repent." But here, the sinner is looked upon as spiritually *dead,* and therefore, in sore need of that which only *God* can impart—"life"! It is here we read of man needing to be "born again" (3:7), needing to be "quickened" (5:21), and needing to be "drawn" (6:44).

9. Neither is the word *"Forgive"* found in John. This, too, is a word often met with in the other Gospels. Why, then, its omission here? In Matt. 9:6 we read, *"The Son of Man* hath power on earth to forgive sins." As Son of Man He "forgives;" as Son of God He bestows "eternal life."

10. No Parables are found in John's Gospel. This is a very notable omission. The key to it is found in Matt. 13: "And the disciples came, and said unto Him, *Why* speakest Thou unto them in parables? He answered and said unto them, Because it is given unto *you* to know the mysteries of the kingdom of heaven, but *to them* it is not given. * * Therefore speak I *to them* in parables: *because* they seeing see not; and hearing they hear not, neither do they understand" (vv. 10-13). Here we learn *why* that Christ, in the later stages of His ministry, taught in "parables." It was to *conceal* from those who had rejected Him, what was comprehensible only to those who had spiritual discernment. But here in John, Christ is not concealing, but *revealing*—revealing God. It is to be deplored that the *rationale* of our Lord's parabolic form of teaching should be known to so few. The popular definition of Christ's parables is that they were earthly stories with a

WHY FOUR GOSPELS?

heavenly meaning. How man gets things upside down! The truth is, that His parables were heavenly stories with an earthly meaning, having to do with His earthly people, in earthly connections. This is another reason why none are found in John—the word in 10:6 is "proverb."

11. In John's Gospel no mention is made of *the Demons*. Why this is we do not know. To say that no reference is here made to them, was, because mention of them would be incompatible with the Divine glories of Christ, hardly seems satisfactory; for, Satan himself is referred to here, again and again. It is, in fact, only here, that the Devil is spoken of three times over as "The prince of this world;" and, Judas, too, as the son of perdition, occupies a more prominent position here than in the other Gospels. Should it be revealed to any of our readers *why* the "demons" are excluded from this Gospel, we shall be very glad to hear from them.

12. There is no account of Christ's *Ascension* in this fourth Gospel. This is very striking, and by implication brings out clearly the Deity of the Lord Jesus. As God the Son He was *omnipresent,* and so, needed not to ascend. As God the Son He fills both heaven and earth. We turn now to,

II. Positive Features of John's Gospel.

1. The Titles of Christ are very significant.

Only here (in the four Gospels) is the Lord Jesus revealed as *"the Word"* (1:1). Only here is He declared to be *the Creator* of all things (1:3). Only here is He spoken of as *"The Only Begotten of the Father"* (1:14). Only here was He hailed as *"The Lamb of God"* (1:29). Only here is He revealed as the great *"I am."* When Jehovah appeared to Moses at the burning bush, and commissioned him to go down into Egypt and demand from Pharaoh the release of His people Israel, Moses said, Who shall I say hath sent me? And God answered, "Thus shalt thou say unto the Children of Israel, *I am* hath sent me unto you" (Ex. 3:14). And here in John's Gospel Christ takes this most sacred title of Deity and appropriates it unto Himself, filling it out with sevenfold fullness: *"I am* the Bread of Life" (6:35); *"I am* the Light of the world" (9:5); *"I am* the Door" (10:7); *"I am* the Good Shepherd" (10:11); *"I am* the Resurrection and the Life" (11:25); *"I am* the Way, the Truth, and the Life" (14:6); *"I am* the true Vine" (15:1).

2. The Deity of Christ is prominently revealed here.

Christ Himself expressly affirmed it: "Verily, verily, I say unto you, The hour is coming, and now is, when the dead shall hear the voice of *the Son of God:* and they that hear shall live" (5:25). Again; "Jesus heard that they had cast him out; and when He had found him, he said unto him, Dost thou believe on *the Son of God?* He answered and said, Who is He, Lord, that I might believe on Him? And Jesus said unto him, Thou hast both seen Him, *and it is He that talketh with thee"* (9:35-37) Once more. "His sisters sent unto Him, saying, Lord, behold, he whom Thou lovest is sick. When Jesus heard that, He said, This sickness is not unto death, but for the glory of God, that *the Son of God* might be glorified thereby" (11:3, 4). Thirty-five times in this Gospel we find the Lord Jesus speaking of God as "My Father." Twenty-five times He here says "Verily, verily" (of a truth, of a truth)—nowhere else found in this intensified form.

Including His own affirmation of it, seven different ones avow His Deity in this Gospel. First, John the Baptist: "And I saw and bare record that this is *the Son of God*" (1:34). Second, Nathaniel, "Rabbi, Thou art *the Son of God*" (1:49). Third, Peter, "And we believe and are sure that Thou art that Christ, *the Son of the living God*" (6:69). The Lord Himself, "Say ye of Him, whom the Father hath sanctified, and sent into the world, Thou blasphemest; because I said, *I am the Son of God*" (10:36). Fifth, Martha, "She saith unto Him, Yea, Lord, I believe that Thou art the Christ, *the Son of God,* which should come into the world" (11:27). Sixth, Thomas, "And Thomas answered and said unto Him, *My Lord and my God*" (20:28). Seventh, the writer of this fourth Gospel, "These are written, that ye might believe that Jesus is the Christ, *the Son of God;* and that believing ye might have life through His name" (20:31).

3. There is a remarkable series of Sevens here.

It is striking to discover how frequently this numeral is found here, and when we remember the significance of this numeral it is even more arresting. Seven is the number of *perfection,* and absolute perfection is not found until we reach *God Himself.* How wonderful, then, that in this Gospel which sets forth the Deity of Christ, the number seven meets us at every turn!

By seven different persons is the Deity of Christ confessed here, and, as we have seen, seven times does He fill out the ineffable "I am" title. John records seven miracles performed by our Lord during His public ministry, no more and no less. Seven times do we read, "These things have I spoken unto you." Seven times did Christ address the woman at the well. Seven times, in John 6, did Christ speak of Himself as "The Bread of Life." Seven things we read of the Good Shepherd doing for His sheep, and seven things Christ says about His sheep in John 10. Seven times does Christ make reference to "the hour" which was to see the accomplishment of the Work given Him to do. Seven times did He bid His disciples pray "in His name." Seven times is the word "hate" found in John 15. There are seven things enumerated in John 16:13, 14 which the Holy Spirit is to do for believers. There were seven things which Christ asked the Father for believers in John 17, and seven times over does He there refer to them as the Father's "gift" to Him. Seven times in this Gospel do we read that Christ declared He spoke only the Word of the Father—7:16; 8:28; 8:47; 12:49; 14:10; 14:24; 17:8. Seven times does the writer of this Gospel refer to himself, without directly mentioning his own name. There are seven important things found in John which are common to all four Gospels. And so we might continue. Let the reader search carefully for himself and he will find many other examples.

4. Man's futile attempts on His life.

Not only was the Christ of God "despised and rejected of men," not only was He "hated without a cause," but His enemies repeatedly sought His life. This feature is noticed, briefly, by the other writers, but John is the only one that tells us *why* their efforts were futile. For example, in John 7:30 we read, "Then they sought to take Him: but no man laid hands on Him, *because His hour was not yet come.*" And again, in 8:20 we read, "These words spake Jesus in the treasury, as He taught in the Temple: and no man laid hands on Him; *for His hour was not yet come."* These Scriptures, in accord with the special character of this fourth Gospel, bring before us the *Divine* side of things. They tell us that the events of earth transpire only according to the *appointment* of Heaven. They show that God is working all things after the counsel of His own will and according to His eternal purpose. They teach us that nothing is left to chance, but that when *God's* "hour" arrives that which has been decreed by His sovereign will, is performed. They reveal the fact that even His enemies are entirely subject to God's immediate control, and that they cannot make a single move without His direct permission.

The Lord Jesus Christ was not the helpless Victim of an angry mob. What He suffered, He endured voluntarily. The enemy might roar against Him, and His emissaries might thirst for His blood, but not a thing could they do without His consent. It is in this Gospel we hear Him saying, "Therefore doth My Father love Me, because I lay down My life, that I might take it again. *No man taketh it from Me,* but I lay it down of Myself. I have power to lay it down, and I have power to take it again" (10: 17, 18). While He hung upon the Cross, His enemies said, "He saved others; *let Him save Himself,* if He be Christ, the Chosen of God" (Luke 23:35). And He accepted their challenge! He saved Himself not *from* death, but *out of it;* not from the Cross, but the Tomb.

5. *The Purpose and Scope of this Gospel.*

The key to it is hung right upon the door. The opening verse intimates that the Deity of Christ is the special theme of this Gospel. The order of its contents is defined in 16:28: 1. "I came forth from the Father:" this may be taken as the heading for the Introductory portion, the first eighteen verses of the opening chapter; 2. "And am come into the world:" this may be taken as the heading for the first main section of this Gospel, running from 1:19 to the end of chapter 12. 3. "Again, I leave the world:" this may be taken as the heading for the second great section of the Gospel, comprising chapters 13 to 17 inclusive, where the Lord is seen apart from "the world," alone with His beloved disciples. 4. "And go to the Father:" this may be taken as the heading for the closing section of this Gospel, made up of its last four chapters, which give us the final scenes, preparatory to the Lord's return to His Father.

The closing verses of John 20 tell us the *purpose* of this Gospel: "And many other signs truly did Jesus in the presence of His disciples, which are not written in this book. But these are written, that ye might believe that Jesus is the Christ, the Son of God; and that believing ye might have life through His name." John's Gospel, then, is peculiarly suited to the unsaved. But this does not exhaust its scope. It is equally fitted for and written to believers; in fact, the opening chapter intimates it is designed specially for the saved, for in 1:16 we read, "And of His fullness *have all we received,* and grace for grace."

6. The Account of His Passion is remarkable.

Here there is no glimpse given us of the Saviour's agony in Gethsemane: there is no crying, "If it be possible let this cup pass from Me," there is no bloody sweat, no angel appearing to strengthen Him.

Here there is no seeking of companionship from His disciples in the Garden; instead, He knows them only as needing *His* protection (see 18:8). Here there is no compelling of Simon to bear His cross. Here there is no mention of the three hours of darkness, nor is reference made to the awful cry, "My God, My God, why hast Thou forsaken Me?" Here there is nothing said of the spectators taunting the dying Saviour, and no mention is made of the insulting challenge of the rulers for Him to descend from the Cross and they would believe in Him. And here there is no word said of the Rending of the Veil, as the Redeemer breathed His last. How striking is this, for in John's Gospel God is *unveiled* throughout; no need, then, for the veil to be rent *here!* John says nothing about Him eating food after the resurrection, for as Son of God, He needed it not!

7. *Christ's dignity and majesty comes out here amid His humiliation.*

John is the only one that tells us that when the Lord's enemies came to arrest Him in the Garden that when He asked them "Whom seek ye?", and they replied, "Jesus of Nazareth," and He then pronounced the sacred "I am," they *"went backward and fell to the ground"* (18:6). What a demonstration of His Godhead was this! How easily could He have walked away unmolested had He so pleased!

John is the only one to speak of His coat "without seam" which the soldiers would not rend (19:24). John is the only one to show us how completely the Saviour was master of Himself—"Jesus *knowing that all things were now accomplished"* (19:28). His mind was not beclouded, nor was His memory impaired. No; even at the close of all His sufferings, the whole scheme of Messianic prediction stood out clearly before Him.

John is the only one of the four Evangelists to record the Saviour's triumphant cry, "It is finished" (19:30), as he is the only one to say that after He had expired the soldier's "brake not His legs" (19:33). John is the only one to tell us of Love's race to the sepulcher (20:3, 4). And John is the only one to say that the risen Saviour "breathed" on the disciples, and said, "Receive ye the Holy Spirit" (20:22).

The closing verse of this Gospel is in perfect keeping with its character and scope. Here, and here only, are we told, "And there are also many other things which Jesus did, the which, if they should be written every one, I suppose that even the world itself could not contain the books that should be written. Amen" (21:25). Thus, the last note here sounded is that of *infinity!*

CONCLUSION

CONCLUSION.

IN our somewhat brief examination of the four Gospels it has been the writer's design to bring before the reader that which is characteristic in each one, pointing out the various connections in which the different Evangelists view our Lord and Saviour. It is evident that each of the Gospels contemplates Him in a distinct relationship —Matthew as King, Mark as Servant, Luke as Son of Man, and John as Son of God. But while each Evangelist portrays the Lord Jesus in an entirely different viewpoint from the others, yet he does not altogether exclude that which is found in the remaining three. God knew that where the Scriptures would be translated into heathen tongues, before the whole Bible or even the complete New Testament was given to different peoples, oftentimes only a single Gospel would be translated as a beginning, and therefore has the Holy Spirit seen to it that each Gospel presents a more or less *complete* setting forth of the manifold glories of His Son. In other words, He caused each writer to combine in his own Evangel the various lines of Truth found in the others, though making these *subordinate* to that which was central and peculiar to himself.

That which is dominant in Matthew's delineation of the Lord Jesus is the presentation of Him as the Son of David, the Heir of Israel's throne, the Messiah and King of the Jews. Yet, while this is the *outstanding* feature of the first Gospel, nevertheless, a careful study of it will discover traces therein of the other offices that Christ filled. Even in Matthew the *Servant* character of our Lord comes into view, though, in an incidental manner. It is Matthew who tells us that when the sons of Zebedee came requesting of Him that they might sit on His right hand and on His left in His kingdom, and that when the other ten apostles were moved with indignation against them, He said, "Ye know that the princes of the Gentiles exercise dominion over them, and that they that are great exercise authority upon them. But it shall not be so among you: but whosoever will be great among you, let him be your minister; and whosoever will be chief among you, let him be your *servant: Even as* the Son of Man came not to be ministered unto, but to minister, and to give His life a ransom for many" (20:25-28); and it is from this Gospel we learn that when He sent forth the Twelve, He warned them, "The disciple is not above his Master, nor the servant above his Lord. It is enough for the disciple that he be as his Master, and the servant as his Lord. If they have called the Master of the house Beelzebub, how much more shall they call them of His household" (10:24, 25).

Again; Matthew's Gospel does not hide from us the *lowly* place the Lord took as *the Son of Man,* for it is *here* we have recorded His word, "The foxes have holes, and the birds of the air have nests; but the Son of Man *hath not where to lay His head*" (8: 20); as it is here we are told that when they that received tribute came to Peter and asked, "Doth your Master pay tribute?" that the Lord said to His disciple, "What thinkest thou, Simon? of whom do the kings of the earth take custom or tribute? of their own children, or of strangers? Peter said unto Him, Of strangers. Jesus said unto him, Then are the children (i. e. of kings) free. Notwithstanding, lest we should offend them, go thou to the sea, and cast an hook, and take up the fish that first cometh up; and when thou hast opened his mouth, thou shalt find a piece of money: that take, and give unto them, *for Me and thee*" (17:25-27)!

So, too, do the *Divine* glories of Christ shine forth on the pages of this first Gospel. It is here that we are told, "Behold, a virgin shall be with Child, and shall bring forth a Son, and they shall call His name Emmanuel, which being interpreted is, *God with us*" (1:23). And it is here we have recorded most fully Peter's notable confession, "Thou art the Christ, *the Son of the living God*" (16:16).

Mark's central purpose is to present Christ as God's perfect Workman yet, here and there, he gives hints that the Servant of Jehovah possessed other and higher glories. This second Gospel, as well as the first and third, record His *Transfiguration* upon the holy mount (9:2), and Mark also tells us of the *Triumphal Entry into Jerusalem* (11:7-10). It is here we are told that when the high priest asked Him, "Art Thou the Christ, the Son of the Blessed?" that He answered, "I am: and ye shall see the Son of Man sitting *on the right hand of power*, and coming in the clouds of Heaven" (14:62). Thus did He bear witness to His Messianic and Kingly glory.

Mark is also careful to tell us in the opening verse of his Gospel that Jesus Christ was *"the Son of God,"* as he also informs us that the demon-possessed man from the tombs cried and said, "What have I to do with Thee, Jesus, Thou *Son of the most high God?*" (5:7). These things do not detract from that which is central in this second Gospel, but guard the Divine glories of Him that "took upon Him the form of a servant."

Luke describes the Humanity of the Saviour, pictures Him as the Son of Man, and shows us the lowly place which He took. But while this is the central theme of the third Gospel, references are also made, here, to His higher glories. It is here we read that the Saviour told the people, "Behold *a greater than Solomon* is here" (11:31), as it is here we also find Him owned as "The Son of David" (18:38). Luke also refers to the Transfiguration and the Triumphal Entry into Jerusalem.

This third Gospel reveals the fact that the Saviour was *more than Man*. It is here we are told that the angel of the Lord said unto Mary, "That Holy Thing which shall be born of thee shall be called *the Son of God*" (1:35); as it is here we also read of the demon-possessed man crying, "What have we to do with Thee Jesus, *Thou Son of God most high*" (8:28)!

So it is with the fourth Gospel. The outstanding feature there is the setting forth of the Deity of Christ, yet a careful reading of John will also reveal His Kingship as well as His Human lowliness. It is here we read of Andrew telling his brother Simon, "We have found *the Messiah,* which is, being interpreted, the Christ (1:41). It is here that we are told Nathaniel owned our Lord as, *"The King of Israel"* (1:49). It is in this fourth Gospel we hear the Samaritans saying unto the converted adulteress, "Now we believe, not because of thy saying: for we have heard Him ourselves, and know that this is indeed *the Christ* (i. e., the Messiah), the Saviour of the world" (4:42). And it is here also we learn that when entering Jerusalem, the people "took branches of palm trees, and went forth to meet Him, and cried, Hosanna, Blessed is *The King of Israel* that cometh in the name of the Lord" (12:13).

In like manner, we find in John illustrations of our Lord's *lowliness*. It is in this fourth Gospel that we read, "Jesus therefore, *being wearied with His journey,* sat thus on the well" (4:6). It is here we find recorded the pathetic fact, that, "every man went unto his own house—Jesus went *unto the mount of Olives*" (7:53; 8:1). Every "man" had his "own house" to which he retired at night, but the Beloved of the Father was a homeless Stranger here! So, again, it is John who tells us, "And it was *winter,* and (being too cold out on the mountain) Jesus walked *in the Temple* in Solomon's porch" (10:22, 23). Once more: it is John who shows us the Lord, as *the perfect Man,* making provision for His widowed mother, providing her a home with His beloved disciple (19:26, 27).

Returning now to our central design in this book, we would take a look at two or three incidents *found in all four Gospels,* and comparing them carefully, would notice the characteristic and distinctive lines in each one. First, let us observe the reference which each Evangelist makes to *John the Baptist.* Matthew alone tells us that he cried, "Repent ye: for *the kingdom* of heaven is at hand" (3:3), for Matthew is the one who presents the Lord Jesus as Israel's King and Messiah. Mark is the only one to tell us that those who were baptized by our Lord's forerunner "confessed their sins" (1:5), this being in accord with the *ministerial* character of this second Gospel. Luke, who dwells on human relationships, is the only writer that tells us about the parentage of the Baptist (chap. 1), as he is the only one to describe in detail the various classes of people who came to him at the Jordan. All of these things are significantly omitted by John, for in this fourth Gospel the emphasis is placed not upon the Baptist, but upon the One he was sent to herald. Here only are we told that he "came to bear witness of the Light" (1:7); that Christ existed before him (1: 15), though as a Child He was born three months after him; and that he testified Christ was both God's "Lamb" (1:29) and God's "Son" (1:34).

Again; let us note what each Evangelist has said about *the Feeding of the five thousand,* and particularly the way in which this miracle is introduced. Matthew says, "And Jesus went forth, and saw a great multitude, and was moved with compassion toward them, and *He healed their sick.* And when it was evening, His disciples came to Him, saying, This is a desert place, and the time is now past; send the multitude away, that they may go into the villages, and buy themselves victuals. But Jesus said unto them, They need not depart; give ye them to eat" (14:14-16). Thus, Matthew prefaces his account of this miracle by speaking of Christ "healing the sick," for this was one of the *Messianic signs.* Mark says: "And Jesus, when He came out, saw much people, and was moved with compassion toward them, because they were as sheep not having a shepherd: and *He began to teach them many things.* And when the day was now far spent, His disciples came unto Him, and said, This is a desert place, and now the time is far passed: Send them away, that they may go into the country round about, and into the villages, and buy themselves bread: for they have nothing to eat. He answered and said unto

WHY FOUR GOSPELS?

them, Give ye them to eat" (6:34-37). Instead of mentioning the "healing of the sick," Mark brings a beautiful *ministerial touch* into his picture by telling us the Saviour was moved with compassion toward the people because they were "as sheep not having a shepherd," and then makes known how the perfect Servant "began to teach them many things," thus *ministering* to them the Word of God. Luke tells us, "And the people, when they knew it, followed Him: and He received them, and spake unto them of the kingdom of God, and healed them *that had need of healing*. And when the day began to wear away, then came the twelve, and said unto Him, Send the multitude away, that they may go into the towns and country round about, and lodge, and get victuals: for we are here in a desert place. But He said unto them, Give ye them to eat" (Luke 9:11-13). Here we find Human sympathy and human want brought out, for Luke presents the great Physician healing, not as a Messianic sign, but healing those "that had *need* of healing." Now, observe, how entirely different is John's method of introducing this miracle. He says nothing about the Messianic sign of healing, nothing about the Servant of God "teaching" the people, and nothing of the Son of Man ministering to the "need" of the sick; instead, he tells us, "When Jesus then lifted up His eyes, and saw a great company come unto Him, He saith unto Philip, Whence shall we buy bread, that these may eat? And He said this to prove him: *for He Himself KNEW what He would do*" (6:5, 6). Thus the fourth Gospel, again, brings out the Deity of Christ, by revealing His Omniscience.

As another example of the characteristic differences of each of the four Evangelists when recording the same or a similar incident, let us take *the Sabbath criticisms* which the Saviour met with. Each of the Gospels make mention of Christ being condemned for transgressing the traditions of the elders with which the Jews had cumbered the Sabbath, and each tells us the reply which He made to His objectors, and the arguments He used to vindicate Himself. In Matt. 12:2, 3 we read, "At that time Jesus went on the Sabbath day through the corn; and His disciples were an hungered, and began to pluck the ears of corn, and to eat. But when the Pharisees saw it, they said unto him, Behold, Thy disciples do that which is not lawful to do upon the Sabbath day." To this our Lord made answer by reminding the Pharisees how that David, when he was an hungered, entered the house of God and did eat the shewbread, sharing it also with those that were with him. Then He went on to say, "Have ye not read in the Law, how that on the Sabbath days the priests in the temple profane the Sabbath, and are blameless? But I say unto you, That in this place *is One greater than the Temple*" (Matt. 12:5, 6). Mark also refers to this same incident, and records part of the reply which the Saviour made on this occasion (see 2:23-28), but it is very striking to observe that he *omits* the Lord's statement that He was "Greater than the Temple." In Luke's Gospel there is a miracle recorded which is not found elsewhere—the healing of the woman who had an infirmity for eighteen years (Luke 13:11-13). As the sequel to this we are told, "And the ruler of the synagogue answered with indignation because that Jesus had healed on the Sabbath day, and said unto the people, There are six days in which men ought to work: in them therefore come and be healed, and not on the

Sabbath" (11:14). But on this occasion we find Christ employed an argument to vindicate Himself, which was thoroughly in keeping with the scope of this third Gospel. "The Lord then answered him, and said, Thou hypocrite, doth not each one of you on the Sabbath loose his ox or his ass from the stall, and lead him away to watering? And ought not this woman, being a daughter of Abraham, whom Satan hath bound, lo, these eighteen years, be loosed from this bond on the Sabbath day?" (13: 15, 16). Here the appeal was not to the Old Testament scriptures, nor to His own Greatness, but to *human sympathies*. John records another miracle, not mentioned by the others, which also met with a similar rebuke from the Lord's foes. But here, in answering His critics, the Lord Jesus vindicated Himself by using an entirely different argument from those employed on other occasions, as noted by other Evangelists. Here we find Him replying: *"My Father* worketh hitherto, *and I work"* (5:17). Thus, we see again, the principle of selection determining what each Evangelist recorded.

One more example must suffice. Let us observe what each Gospel says about *the Arrest in the Garden*. Matthew tells us, "And while He yet spake, lo, Judas, one of the twelve, came, and with him a great multitude with swords and staves, from the chief priests and elders of the people. Now he that betrayed Him gave them a sign, saying, Whomsoever I shall kiss, that same is He: hold Him fast. And forthwith he came to Jesus, and said, Hail, Master; and kissed Him. And Jesus said unto him, Friend, wherefore art thou come? Then came they, and laid hands on Jesus, and took Him. And, behold, one of them which was with Jesus stretched out his hand, and drew his sword, and struck a servant of the high priest's, and smote off his ear. Then said Jesus unto him, Put up thy sword again unto his place: for all they that take the sword shall perish with the sword. Thinkest thou that I cannot now pray to My Father, and He shall presently give Me more than twelve legions of angels? But how then shall the Scriptures be fulfilled, that thus it must be?" (26:47-54). Mark says: "And immediately, while He yet spake, cometh Judas, one of the twelve, and with him a great multitude with swords and staves, from the chief priests and the scribes and the elders. And he that betrayed Him had given them a token, saying, Whomsoever I shall kiss, that same is He; take Him, and lead Him away safely. And as soon as he was come, he goeth straightway to Him, and saith, Master, Master; and kissed Him. And they laid their hands on Him, and took Him. And one of them that stood by drew a sword, and smote a servant of the high priest, and cut off his ear. And Jesus answered and said unto them, Are ye come out as against a thief, with swords and with staves to take Me? I was daily with you in the Temple teaching, and ye took Me not: but the Scriptures must be fulfilled" (14:43-49). It will be observed that Mark omits the fact that Christ addressed the traitor as "Friend" (see Ps. 41:9—Messianic prophecy), as he also says nothing about His right to ask the Father for twelve legions of angels. In Luke we read, "And while He yet spake, behold a multitude, and he that was called Judas, one of the twelve, went before them, and drew near unto Jesus to kiss Him. But Jesus said unto him, Judas, betrayest thou the Son of Man with a kiss? When they that were about Him, saw what would follow, they said

WHY FOUR GOSPELS? 183

unto Him, Lord, shall we smite with the sword? and one of them smote the servant of the high priest, and cut off his right ear. Then Jesus answered and said, Suffer ye thus far. And He touched his ear, and healed him. Then Jesus said unto the chief priests, and captains of the temple, and the elders, which were come unto Him, Be ye come out, as against a thief, with swords, and staves? When I was daily with you in the Temple, ye stretched forth no hands against Me, but this is your hour, and the power of darkness" (Luke 22:47-53). Luke is the only one to record Christ's touching but searching question to Judas, as he is the only one to tell us of Christ healing the ear of the high priest's servant. Entirely different is John's account. In 18:3 we read, "Judas then, having received a band of men and officers from the chief priests and Pharisees, cometh thither with lanterns and torches and weapons." But here only is it added, "Jesus therefore, knowing all things that should come upon Him, went forth, and said unto them, Whom seek ye. They answered Him, Jesus of Nazareth." Here only are we told, "Jesus said unto them, I am. And Judas also, which betrayed Him, stood with them. As soon then as He had said unto them, I am, they went backward, and fell to the ground" (18:5, 6). Here only do we read, "If therefore ye seek Me, let these go their way: that the saying might be fulfilled, which He spake, Of them which Thou gavest Me have I lost none" (18:8, 9). And here only are we told that the Lord said to the disciple who had cut off the ear of the priest's servant, "Put up thy sword into the sheath: the cup which *My Father hath given Me, shall I not drink it?*" (John 18:11).

In closing, we would call attention to one other

feature of the Gospels, that has often been noticed by others, and that is, what is found in the closing portions of the respective Gospels. There is a striking and climactic order observed. At the close of Matthew's Gospel, we read of *the Resurrection of Christ* (28:1-8). At the close of Mark's Gospel, we read of *the Ascension of Christ* (16:19). At the close of Luke's Gospel, we hear of *the Coming of the Holy Spirit* (24:49). While at the close of John's Gospel, reference is made to *the Return of Christ* (21:21-23)! May that Day soon dawn when He shall come again to receive us unto Himself, and in the little interval that yet awaits, may we study His Word more diligently and obey its precepts more carefully.

APPENDIX

Dispensationalism
by Arthur W. Pink
[*from "Studies in the Scriptures," August, 1948*]

Occasionally a brief reference is made in these pages to the crudities and absurdities of what is termed "Dispensationalism," for some of our readers have been influenced by its evil teaching, and it becomes a duty to seek to remove this stumbling-stone from their path. Others of our friends, though unacquainted with this erroneous system, need to be warned against the same. The movement was born a century ago, and has been proudly advertised and extensively propagated under the guise of "new light on God's Word," an opening up of "the deeper things of God." It is a system of *interpreting the Scriptures:* an unwarrantable method of segregating its contents, which, if adopted, *robs* God's people of much of His Word. Not content with rightly distinguishing between what pertained unto those under the old and new covenants, and between what is spoken to the "saints" and to "the children of disobedience," Old and New Testament alike are broken up into sections and labelled "for the Jew," "for the Gentiles," "for the Church of God," and most of it "NOT to *us.*" These modern Jehoikims (Jer. 36:23) sever one passage from another, as they are arbitrarily alleged to belong to different dispensations or eras, both in the past and in the future.

Though posing as men of exceptional insight, as "profound Bible teachers," the Dispensationalists are far from being agreed among themselves as to how many separate eras are treated of in Scripture, or at what precise point one ends and another begins. Some claim there are but seven, others twelve, while a few make them to be fourteen. The popular Scofield Bible teaches there are no fewer than four covered by the book of Genesis alone, and that a fifth starts in Exodus 19, under which God dealt with men on entirely different lines. Dr. S. says: "A dispensation is a period of time during which man is tested in respect of obedience to some specific revelation of the will of God." The first he styles "The Dispensation of Innocency," which "ended in the judgment of the Expulsion (Gen. 3:24)." The second "Conscience," which "ended in the judgment of the Flood." The third "Human Government," and "the judgment of the confusion of tongues ended the *racial* testing." The fourth "Promise," which "ended when Israel rashly accepted the Law." The fifth "Law," which "extends from Sinai to Calvary."

Now the Greek word *oikonomia,* meaning "house arrangement," occurs seven times in the New Testament. The first three in Luke 16:2, 3, 4, where it is rendered "stewardship," which connotes something radically different from an *era!* In no instance does the *time-element* enter into the signification of the word! In I Corinthians 9:17, Paul declared "a dispensation of the Gospel is committed unto me": how utterly absurd would it be to conclude that an "age" had been entrusted to him!—rather was it an evangelical stewardship or economy. "If ye have heard of the dispensation of the grace of God which is *given me* to you-ward " (Eph. 3:2), "whereof I was made a minister according to the dispensation of God which is *given to me* for you" (Col 1:25). In neither of those verses is there the remotest reference to a section of history, but rather to an evangelical administration. As the business of a steward is to serve and distribute, so the apostle was called to *dispense* the Gospel to the Gentiles, to communicate to others what God had revealed to him. In Ephesians 1:10—the only other reference—the simple meaning is that God's plan or economy of salvation is to concentrate all in Christ, all the redeemed being united to one Head. Thus, the Scriptural usage of the word "dispensation" signifies *not* an age or era, *but* a stewardship or administration of things received by commission.

What Scriptural authority, it may be asked, do the Dispensationalists have for their startling method of exegesis?—one quite unknown to the Reformers and godly Puritans! To what passages do they point as warrant for their emphatic assertion that the greater part of the Bible pertains not to those living in this Christian era?—wrongly denominated by them "the Dispensation of Grace." Wrongly, we say, for as a distinguishing title it is utterly misleading, seeing that God dealt in pure grace with all He chose in Christ, from the time of Abel until the day of Pentecost: *see* Genesis 6:8; Exodus 33:12; Jeremiah 31:2; Psalm 84:11; Proverbs 3:34; Nehemiah 9:31; Jonah 4:2. Surely some very plain and emphatic "thus saith the Lord" is required by believers today when they are dogmatically informed that the whole of the Old Testament and much of the New has no direct reference to them. But no such Divine authorization is forthcoming: nothing but an appeal to the *sound* of one verse, and a human *guess* upon another!

The first passage to which they have recourse is, "Study to show thyself approved unto God, a workman that needeth not to be ashamed, *rightly dividing* the Word of Truth." (II Tim 2:15), which they affirm to mean partitioning one part to this dispensation and another to that. Let it be duly noted that this verse is not an exhortation to God's people at large, telling them how to handle His Word; but, instead, part of the instructions given to a minister of the Gospel; nor is there any intimation in the context that the Spirit was about to enunciate a revolutionizing principle for interpreting the Scriptures. If this verse be compared with Matthew 7:6; John 16:12; I Corinthians 3:2, etc., its meaning is clear. The occupant of the pulpit is to give diligence in becoming equipped to give his hearers "their *portion* of meat in due season (Luke 12:42). For him to "rightly divide the Word" is to minister it *suitably* to the cases and circumstances of his congregation—to sinners and saints, the indifferent and inquiring, babes and fathers, the tempted and afflicted, the backslider and the fallen.

The remaining passage is Luke 4:16-20, where in the synagogue of Nazareth Christ read Isaiah 61:1, and for some reason or other stopped in the middle of verse 2. The unauthorized *guess* of the Dispensationalists is that our Lord omitted the next words "and the day of vengeance of our God" (almost always ignoring the additional "to comfort all that mourn"!) because *that* pertained to a future and distant era. Scofield's Bible says, "Jesus stopped at 'the acceptable year of the Lord,' which is connected with the first advent and the dispensation of grace; 'the day of vengeance of our God' belongs to the second advent and judgment." Thus we are asked to believe that Isaiah 61:2, treats of two totally different "dispensations" and that the word "and" in the middle of it covers a period which has already extended for more than nineteen centuries! Anything more bizarre and ridiculous could scarcely be imagined. *Facts refute it!* Did not Christ plainly proclaim "the day of the vengeance of our God" when He asserted "and thou Capernaum, which art exalted unto heaven, shalt be brought down to hell"? when He pronounced "woe" after "woe" upon the scribes and Pharisees? when He declared to the Jewish nation "Behold! your house is left unto you desolate"? when He announced of the temple "there shall not be left here one stone upon another"? He *did* as certainly as He also comforted all that mourned with a godly sorrow.

On those two verses (II Tim 2:15; Isa. 61:2) has been based an entire system of interpreting the Scriptures, which is claimed to be essential to their right understanding and apportioning. *That is all* the support which this fanciful theory has! Never was so imposing a structure erected upon so flimsy a foundation. Never were credulous simpletons so easily beguiled as when they believed the *ipsi dixit* of these exegetical thieves and suffered themselves to be deprived of much of God's Word by accrediting their assertions that much in the Prophets is "Millennial," that the Sermon on the Mount belongs to "the Kingdom age," and that most of the Revelation treats only of "the Tribulation period." Cease ye from man! Receive the whole Bible as God's Word *to* you and *for* you.

As a sample of the pernicious teaching of the Scofield Bible on this subject, we cite a part of its note on John 1:18: "As a Dispensation, grace begins with the death and resurrection of Christ (Rom. 3: 24-26; 6:24, 25). The point of testing is no longer legal obedience as the condition of salvation, but acceptance or rejection of Christ," etc. It betrays the greatest ignorance to assert that sinners were saved in a different way under the Mosaic economy. Limiting ourselves to the Psalms, we there see that there was then *the same* conviction of guilt and demerit (32:3-5), the same inevitable condemnation on the ground of God's Law (143:2), the same earnest crying for undeserved mercy (51:1), faith in His revealed character as a just God and Saviour (25:8), hope of pardon, resting on propitiation (130:7), pleading of God's name or glory of all His perfections (25:11), joy and peace in believing (89:15, 16), trust in God's faithfulness to His promises (89:1, 2), confidence in the righteousness of Another (84:9), disowning of all ground for boasting (115:1) as there is now! Thus the *same Gospel* which was "preached unto Abraham" (Gal. 3:8), was proclaimed and believed in the days of David, and Jewish sinners were no more saved then by "legal obedience" than are Gentile sinners today. "*All* Scripture is given by inspiration of God, and is profitable for doctrine" (II Tim 3:16). Every part is needed by us: let none filch any from you.

www.ingramcontent.com/pod-product-compliance
Lightning Source LLC
Chambersburg PA
CBHW071423160426
43195CB00013B/1784